How to Handle Worry
A Catholic Approach

Marshall J. Cook

BOOKS & MEDIA

Boston

Library of Congress Cataloging-in-Publication Data

Cook, Marshall, 1944–
    How to handle worry : a Catholic approach / Marshall J. Cook.
      p. cm.
    ISBN 0-8198-3379-7
    1. Christian life—Catholic authors. 2. Worry—Religious aspects
—Catholic Church. 3. Peace of mind—Religious aspects—Catholic
Church. I. Title.
BX2350.2.C6138 1999
248.8'6—dc21   99–25895
                                                     CIP

Cover design: Helen Rita Lane, FSP

Printed and published in the U.S.A. by Pauline Books & Media, 50 Saint Pauls Avenue, Boston MA 02130-3491.

www.pauline.org

Pauline Books & Media is the publishing house of the Daughters of St. Paul, an international congregation of women religious serving the Church with the communications media.

1 2 3 4 5 6   04 03 02 01 00 99

"Consider the lilies of the field, how they grow; they neither toil nor spin, yet I tell you, even Solomon in all his glory was not clothed like one of these." —Matthew 6:28

Contents

Foreword 9

Preface 11

Introduction 13

1. Bringing Our Burdens to God 17

2. "Good" and "Bad" Worry:
   How to Tell Them Apart 21

3. The Difference between Faith
   and Positive Thinking 29

4. Time Management Didn't Save Us—
   How Faith Can Heal Speed Sickness 38

5. Don't Sweat the Small Stuff 47

6. Continuing the Faith Journey
   and the Worry Journal 51

7. Meeting Worry Head On 56

8. Moving from Feeling to Doing 61

9. How the Prayer Card
   Can Defeat Five Kinds of Worry 66

10. How Are We to Pray? 73

11. Maintaining the Temple of the Spirit 77

12. Five Ways to Get Worry to Work for You 82

13. On the Next Oprah...Me!—
    A Chance to Practice What I Preach 85

14. Don't Get Mad. Don't Get Even. Get Peace 89

15. Seeking Mercy Instead of Justice 94

16. Accepting the Inevitable 98

17. Surrendering to Faith/Fear 103

18. Living Faith/Fear on a Cold Day in January 106

Foreword

During my father's nine month illness, I struggled with fear and anxieties. At times, I felt overwhelmed, almost crippled with fright. Luckily, my God, my family and my friend Marshall pulled me through. My dear friend lent me (or did I steal it?) the manuscript of this book. It was a wonderful gift. His words flipped on the light of hope and helped me cope with my demons. Marshall takes a probing look at what kills our joys and paralyzes our spirit, and how faith can help us. Whether he is talking about giving speeches or sweating out illnesses, Marshall provides practical insight and wisdom. He uses the power of Scripture to sort out answers to our everyday stresses. "Perfect love casts out fear" (1 Jn 4:18). This book is a snippet from that perfect love, a perfect book for folks seeking peace of mind.

Jack Walsh
Townsend, MA
April, 1999

Preface

A Brief Note about Your Author, an "Expert" on Worry

I've taught for the University of Wisconsin Outreach for sixteen years, conducting about sixty workshops a year on developing creativity, handling stress and anxiety, and putting thoughts and feelings on paper. I speak at conferences and seminars all across the country. I've written four books on writing, one on stress management, and one on the hometown. I edit a newsletter for writers.

When I approach the podium in some faraway city, clutching my handouts and overheads, the moderator introduces me as an "expert." Folks look to me for answers. They honor me by spending their precious time listening to me. So I'd better be an expert.

But I'm no Ted Williams expert. I'm a Charlie Lau expert.

Ted Williams hit .344 over nineteen seasons in major league baseball, which is way better than good. He hit 521 home runs, also an extraordinary mark. In 1941 he batted .406, making him the last player to hit over .400 for a full season. Williams is surely an expert on hitting; he could do it better than anyone who ever lived.

That's not the kind of expert I am.

Charlie Lau batted just .255 over eleven seasons in the majors and hit just sixteen home runs. And yet, perhaps because he worked so hard and thought so much about hitting, Lau became an outstanding hitting instructor. Whenever he sets out to teach a team to hit better, the team hits better. He has a system, and he works hard to explain it effectively, so others can put it to good use.

If I'm any kind of an expert, I'm a Charlie Lau kind of expert. I know how to identify and deal with anxiety. I *know* worry, and I'm learning each day how to let faith defeat fear.

Writing is a tool of discovery for me. This will be our mutual exploration as we learn to confront and overcome our fears. Our fears are different; our strategies will be different. But we will share the journey.

"We know that all things work for good for those who love God, who are called according to his purpose" (Rom 8:28).

Introduction

The Paradox of the Anxious Christian

The day I was born, American troops pushed across the border into Belgium, my father's homeland, to liberate it from the Nazis. A few months later, my country dropped an atomic bomb on Hiroshima.

I grew up in the shadow of the San Gabriel Mountains of southern California. Altadena was a peaceful little town then, dotted with orange groves, horse ranches and poppy fields. But life could be scary, even in my peaceful little hometown. I dreamt a witch was shaking my bed and woke up to find that an earthquake, not a witch, had shaken me loose from my childhood dreams. I stood on my front porch, ashes raining down on me, and watched as fire crested my beloved mountain and began to rampage down the slope toward me.

What was it in your hometown—typhoons, hurricanes, droughts, floods, ice storms? Every hometown has its share of natural disasters.

Luther Burbank Elementary School was full of frightening natural phenomena, too—other children and teachers. The kids teased me, of course. (I didn't know they teased everyone.) Marauding gangs spread terror on the playground—yes, even in 1950, and even in first grade. The teachers were kind enough, I'm sure, but they were giants, and they made demands on me I wasn't at all sure I could meet.

Teasing, taunting and tests would have been terrifying enough without the "drop drills" spawned by the dawning of the age of nuclear weapons. Without warning, a teacher would suddenly yell "Drop!" and we would scramble under our desks, bumping heads and scraping knees. We had to huddle, arms over our heads, until given the all-clear. Then we would go back to our arithmetic problems or silent reading.

Monsters gave way to mushroom clouds in my nightmares. But you had nightmares, too, didn't you? All children get them. It's part of growing up.

I reached puberty, and the Russians launched Sputnik. I'm sure there's no causal link here, but they did occur at about the same time.

Khrushchev took off his shoe, pounded it on the table at the United Nations, and vowed to bury us. Missiles bearing nuclear warheads sprouted on Cuban soil, just ninety miles from our shores. But the news brought the most violent images—pictures of black people being assaulted with fire hoses, threatened with dogs, and beaten with clubs, not in some faraway country but in the America I pledged allegiance to at school and vowed to do my best for at Scout meetings.

Add in the terror of trying to get up the nerve to ask a girl out on a date, of having to perform on the parallel bars in PE class, of facing one of Mr. Sheinkopf's killer world history tests or one of Senor Reyes' Spanish dictations, and you have the portrait of a young man in a perpetual state of anxiety, punctuated by frequent rushes of downright terror.

Even when nothing specific frightened me, I was plagued by anxieties I came to call the "formless furies." They chased me through each day and caught me when I closed my eyes at night. I would feel the jolt of adrenaline, the painful thudding of my heart, the swirl of confused and chaotic thoughts. Scenarios of disaster played nightly in the theater of my mind. I couldn't sleep, and I worried about not sleeping.

The paradox of the faith-filled, fearful Christian

While I was growing up scared, I was also growing up Christian. I went to church every Sunday, and I *believed*. I prayed with fervor and felt God's daily presence in my life.

Later, out of an adolescent desire to reject my parents' faith, I pursued Buddhism but couldn't convince my heart to stop caring about the world. In college I embraced existentialism, facing the abyss of life's essential meaninglessness. But again my heart wouldn't buy what my head was trying to sell it; I felt meaning and purpose underlying life.

I reaffirmed my belief in a loving God who gave us his only begotten Son, so that we might have life in abundance for eternity in his presence. I believed then, and I believe now, that Jesus Christ is the living Son of the living God and that Christ's death on the cross redeemed us, gaining for us a salvation we no more deserve than we deserve the gift of life on earth. I converted to Catholicism, the faith of my father's people and of my heart, and my faith deepened and flourished in the rich ritual and nourishing banquet of the Eucharist.

I protested against our government's involvement in Vietnam, filed for conscientious objector status, got fired from my first teaching job—all in a perpetual state of anxiety. Assassins cut down Bobby Kennedy, Martin Luther King Jr. and John Kennedy. Their deaths devastated me. Chaos seemed to rule; yet faith survived.

How could this be? How could terror and trust coexist? How could I actively believe in and enthusiastically worship a loving God and still suffer from crippling anxiety? And how, with faith and anxiety having coexisted in me for so many years, was I finally able to begin to allow faith to overcome the fear?

More importantly, if you struggle with the same sort of duality as a faith-filled but fearful Christian, how can *you* allow such a healing to occur in your life?

These fundamental questions have propelled this book into being. We'll seek our answers together, exploring the path that leads us away from anxiety and toward the peace God promises us.

We've backed away from the chilling edge of nuclear war and seen the fall of the Iron Curtain. We've made incredible advances in the battle against many diseases. But each week brings news of famine and war in another part of the world. A deadly and mysterious disease called AIDS stalks us. Sexual assault and child abuse are daily topics in the press. Our "entertainment" often overflows with violence. The world is still a scary place.

But by facing and naming our fears, using the guidance of Scripture, and opening our hearts to God's healing love, we can strive to live in faith and trust, freed from needless anxiety.

"God is spreading grace around the world like a five-year-old spreads peanut butter; thickly, sloppily, eagerly, and if we are in the back shed trying to stay clean, we don't even get a taste" (Donna Schaper, Stripping Down: The Art of Spiritual Restoration*).*

---

1   Bringing Our Burdens to God

We gather at Mass to praise God and to celebrate the miracle of the death and resurrection of Jesus Christ. But my, don't we seem awfully calm about the whole thing?

Some of us mumble our way through the responses, sink into a coma during the homily, stare vacantly while others sing the hymns, start shrugging into coats and gloves before the final blessing.

How can this be? We're there because we want to be, *need* to be—aren't we?

Driving through central California one summer afternoon, I heard a radio evangelist say, "If we really believed what we say we believe, they couldn't keep us away from church with shotguns." That image stunned me. I was dimly aware that, in some countries of the world, they probably *did* use guns to keep the people from attending church. Yet we speak of the *obligation*, not the *opportunity*, to attend Mass.

"If we *really* believed," the radio preacher concluded, "we'd have to wear crash helmets to church, because we'd be bouncing off the walls!" I haven't seen many helmets at Mass lately, have you?

At that "obligatory" Sunday Mass, we dare to ask God to

"protect us from all anxiety, as we wait in joyful hope for the coming of the Lord." Do we mean it? Do we believe that God will do it?

Surely our belief is imperfect and unfinished. The cry of the father of the child with the unclean spirit is our cry, too: "I do believe, help my unbelief!" (Mk 9:24). But shouldn't even an imperfect faith in God's perfect love protect us from the corrosive anxiety that can rob life of its joy?

"Do not be afraid; just have faith," Jesus told the ruler of the synagogue, whose daughter had just died (Mk 5:36). Why can't it be that simple for us?

It can, but it won't be easy. The most simple truths are the most elusive.

In the chapters that follow we'll explore Christ's teaching about worry—and our own reaction to these clear, simple truths. As we do, we'll discover together how to let our faith overcome our fear.

We'll explore worry as a universal part of the human condition, examining the difference between useful worry—the kind that enables us to avoid danger and prepare for future trials—and the senseless anxiety that paralyzes us by robbing us of energy and will.

We will trace worry to its roots, learn why we cling to our worries, and come to understand that the behaviors we adopt to try to ease the pain of anxiety may in fact intensify and perpetuate that anxiety.

We'll look at the ways our society fosters and nurtures our fears. We will explore the limits of positive thinking and see why time management might actually increase our anxiety.

Since worry often becomes so automatic it feels like instinct, which is to say it doesn't "feel" at all, we'll learn how to catch ourselves in the act of worrying, so that we can choose another alternative.

We will honor the "unacceptable" experience of anxiety and work through it instead of trying to evade our fear. We'll face and name our demons, giving them tangible shape and substance.

We'll explore five specific brands of worry, stemming from five diverse sources, and will see how to defeat all five kinds—and any other exotic strain we might encounter. (Like evil spirits and the flu virus, worry's name is Legion.) We will even learn how to lessen the impact of the most persistent worries by scheduling specific prayer times for them.

Worry often becomes so automatic
it feels like instinct.

————<◆>————

With Martha, we can learn to put aside our chores and live wholly in the moment, in communion with Jesus. This will let us stop "sweating the small stuff" and show us how to give the "big stuff" to God.

We'll learn to accept the inevitable and let go of the past. We'll renounce revenge in favor of forgiveness, eliminating a major source of anxiety in our lives.

Faith can heal us of anxiety. As we let it, we'll re-encounter the central paradox of our faith, the notion that we must willingly lose our lives to find them. We'll learn the power and freedom to be found in a conscious surrendering to God's will and God's possibilities for us, as manifested in his Word and in his world.

Learning at last to escape from needless anxiety will require time and effort. Are you ready to make that kind of commitment?

A woman was trying to decide whether to enroll in a masters degree program in pastoral ministries. "Going part time, it will take me five years," she lamented. "I'll be forty before I finish!"

"And how old will you be in five years," a wise friend responded, "if you don't take the program?"

When you reach the end of this book, you won't be finished or "cured." The work will continue. You'll live your faith and confront your worry every day, and every day your faith will become stronger, and anxiety will lose a bit more of its hold on you.

Your journey from fear to faith is the work of a lifetime. Pick yourself up every time you fall. Forgive yourself every time you fail.

Pick yourself up every time you fall.
Forgive yourself every time you fail.

————<◆>————

"Don't be afraid; just have faith." It really is that simple. It's just going to take time and effort to grow into a better understanding of that simplicity, an understanding that involves all of you, intellect and intuition, logic and emotion, and reaches into your soul.

"My life is mostly a struggle for survival. Not a holy struggle, but an anxious struggle resulting from the mistaken idea that it is the world that defines me" (Henri J. M. Nouwen, The Return of the Prodigal Son).

---

2   "Good" and "Bad" Worry: How to Tell Them Apart

"Often I am like a small boat on the ocean," Nouwen wrote, "completely at the mercy of the waves." Ever have that feeling? Do you have it a lot? Then worry, by whatever name—fear, anxiety, angst—is a problem for you. The feeling of being powerless, of being buffeted by fate, is robbing you of your ability to deal with your challenges and to rejoice in God's gift of life.

Worry is a waste of time and energy, a real life-snatcher. It hides in the shadows, disrupts your rest, damages your ability to make decisions and steals the pleasure and satisfaction you should derive from work and play.

When we worry, we aren't planning, working toward a goal, or thinking constructively. We're obsessing about a problem, imagining the worst, failing to make decisions, avoiding action.

Worry ignores the present to fuss over a future that never comes. Worry rejects the sweet gift of *now* to chase the ever-receding horizon of *then*. Worry substitutes for *do*, and evades *yes*.

Worrying is like paying interest on a debt. You have

nothing to show for it; you still have to pay back the principal, and you have no money left for the things you really need. Substitute energy and enthusiasm for money and you understand what worry does to you.

*Worry ignores the present
to fuss over a future that never comes.*

———————<◆>———————

But not all worry is harmful. Worry is a natural, inevitable, even a productive part of life. We just need to figure out where to draw the line.

"To live is to worry," Dr. C. W. Saleeby wrote way back in 1907. "The cause of worry is life; its cure is death." Saleeby noted that worry springs from our desire to live and our desire to be happy. If we care, we worry. Worry has been common to all races and in all times, a natural state of conscious living.

"To venture causes anxiety," philosopher Soren Kierkegaard noted over a century ago, "but not to venture is to lose oneself." He called anxiety "our best teacher" and linked it to the freedom to choose among possibilities. Anxiety, he wrote, is "the dizziness of freedom." "He...who has learned rightly to be anxious," he concluded, "has learned the most important thing."

Psychologist Rollo May likened anxiety to "the zest of the racehorse at the starting gate." He observed that persons with more originality and creativity often feel more anxiety.

In his controversial bestseller, *Listening to Prozac*, Peter Kramer took the notion of good worry a step further. "What links men and women to God," Kramer wrote, "is precisely their guilt, anxiety, and loneliness."

"And what would we be, we sinful creatures, without fear?" asked Jorge, the old blind monk in Umberto Eco's *The Name of the Rose*. He called fear "perhaps the most foresighted, the most loving of the divine gifts."

Our fear, specifically our fear of death, gives life its meaning and focus, wrote psychologist/angler Paul Quinnett in a remarkable book called *Pavlov's Trout*. After asserting that we all fear death, he continued:

> To fish fully, we must fish in the face of death. This is good, not bad. To relish life means to know and to feel that it is always ending, not just for others, but for ourselves, too.... It is this awareness of life following death that lends a wonderful, bittersweet taste to a perfect day on a perfect stream, and gives authenticity to our angling.

And Saleeby asserted: "Unselfish worry has been one of the saving forces of history, one of the greatest friends of mankind."

But confronting all our possibilities can lead us, not to freedom and positive action, but to retreat and denial. Rather than liberating our energies, anxiety can paralyze our will, sap us of our energy, or express itself in compulsive and self-destructive activity.

Our goal, then, as we explore our worries and God's teaching about worry, will not be to eliminate all anxiety. That isn't possible, and it wouldn't be good even if it were possible. The well-lived life embraces concern for ourselves and for others, some reasonable amount of "good worry." We will work, instead, to eliminate the negative, destructive "bad worry."

But how will we know the difference?

Suppose that two athletes experience anxiety before a big game. The first uses the fear to help focus his concentration and funnel his energy into the task at hand. The second athlete lets fear dominate him. His muscles turn to jelly, and anxiety destroys his performance. Same fear; opposite results.

Jerry West was the first kind of athlete. Through his college basketball career at West Virginia and as an all-pro guard for the Los Angeles Lakers, he earned the nickname "Mister Clutch." His teammates wanted him to take the last shot with the game on the line. More importantly, he wanted the ball in his hands at those crucial moments. He made the "normal" shots, the ones you're supposed to make, even under intense pressure. Occasionally he made the "abnormal" ones, once sending a playoff game against the Boston Celtics into overtime by hitting a buzzerbeating shot from well beyond half court.

Fear can sharpen the senses or paralyze them. Fear can raise our awareness of and vigilance toward threats, or it can lead to inappropriate behavior, apathy, or paralysis of the will.

Anxiety may awaken you in the midst of night, on fire with an idea, a vision, the solution to a problem. Nervous energy, focused and purposeful, drives you from the warm bed—to create a masterpiece, to pray with passion, maybe just to change the kitty litter—but with such gusto!

Or that same predawn anxiety alarm may find you wide-eyed and paralyzed with panic, the God-light of your creativity focused, not on the goal or vision, but on vivid images of disaster. If you act at all, your actions may degenerate into compulsive behavior, temporarily soothing the anxiety but never touching the true cause—so that you have to keep performing the action again and again.

In both cases, you're awake when you want to be sleeping. But you may benefit from the first disturbance and dread the second.

It's that second kind of anxiety, the crippling, hurtful kind, that we're stalking.

"Good" anxiety produces an appropriate and proportionate response. For example:

- A car cuts you off in traffic. Before you can consciously react, you have swerved into the median divide, missing oncoming traffic by inches. You feel awful—terror produces a vicious hangover—but you're alive.

- The neighbor's dog snarls and bares its teeth. You back out of range, before you have time to debate the socially acceptable response.

- It's your turn to lead the weekly Scripture study, and you're plain scared. But you fight your way through the first few sentences, and the icy anxiety dissolves.

Such responses seem normal, don't they? We might even wonder and worry if we didn't have them.

But "bad" anxiety may produce a response totally out of proportion to the threat. For example:

- The driver of the car behind you honks because you fail to respond instantly to a green light. Enraged, you suppress the urge to leap from your car and confront the miscreant. But you seethe about the "incident" for hours or even days.

- The neighbor's miniature Schnauzer yips from the window as you walk by on the sidewalk; you feel convulsed by terror and consider packing a gun the next time you take a walk around the block.

- You turn down the invitation to join that Scripture study, even though you know you'd really benefit, because the thought of sharing your thoughts with others creates such intense panic in you.

We might call these reactions excessive or inappropriate. But we'd better be careful about judging the "appropriateness" of anybody's reactions. When Jesus advised us to "judge not," he was making practical as well as moral sense. We can never know enough to judge another person accurately.

There is no "normal" tolerance level for anxiety, no "normal" reaction to danger or stress. You have your own internal standards. If your behavior seems like a problem to you, then it is a problem, *your* problem. You need to seek your solution in prayer and Scripture study, and possibly through professional help.

We can never know enough
to judge another person accurately.

———<•>———

We know the tree by the fruit it bears. Good worry results in productive activity and a balanced life of rest, work and play, a productive partnership of faith and acts. Bad worry cripples the will and leads to ineffectual activity or no activity at all.

But productivity alone isn't a reliable guideline. Bad worry can drive us to frantic levels of activity. These efforts may gain for us certain rewards—a good job, a high salary, the respect of our peers—while tearing us up inside and building a towering wall between us and God.

If anxiety pushes you into workaholism, your boss may reward you, and colleagues may learn to rely on your sacrifices. Your family may appreciate and depend on the financial security and comfortable lifestyle your work produces. But you may shrivel and die inside, maintaining an energetic, competent persona right up to the breakdown.

How much is too much?

Anxiety comes from stress, an internal reaction to life's pressures and challenges. External stressors—a demanding job, an unreasonable boss, a sick or dying loved one, a troubled child, the need to work two jobs to keep the family going—trigger internal stress.

Your level of stress depends on how many stressors you're dealing with and how long you have to deal with them. Anxiety hinges on how you deal with your stress. If the stressor doesn't go away, and if you don't deal with it positively, anxiety builds.

Any change, even good change, creates stress and anxiety. Getting married, gaining a promotion at work, even winning the lottery can be as stressful as family problems or getting fired or going deeply into debt. Holidays and vacations can be stressful, because they overtax our energies and abilities and because we're *supposed* to be having a wonderful time, no matter how we're really feeling.

Often we can't do much about the stressors. But we can do a great deal about the amount of internal stress we allow them to cause in us.

Hans Selye conducted early research into the consequences of stress. In one famous experiment, he put mice in a refrigerator to see how they would react to the stress of numbing but not lethal cold. (My family and I conducted the same experiment by moving from California to Wisconsin in 1979.)

Invariably the reaction followed three distinctive stages. First, the mice hunkered down, huddled together, and sulked. (Lots of folks do that their first winter in Wisconsin, too.) But they soon got busy, building nests, discovering food sources, acting cooperatively to cope with their challenging environment.

So far, so good. But we need to pay special attention to the third stage. After a period of cooperative, productive activity, the refrigerated mice invariably died. Stress literally killed them—just as we're now learning that it can kill us—

through a variety of ailments stemming from the suppression of the immune system. Too much stress, experienced over too long a time, can hurt us physically, psychologically, spiritually.

Just as too much stress can harm us, too little stress, Selye concluded from this and other experiments, can cause lethargy, boredom, even depression and despair. If we aren't challenged we feel useless, and life lacks meaning. Just enough stress, a state Selye called "eustress," keeps us happily productive while allowing us enough time for rest and recreation.

So how much is too much and how much is just enough stress for you? Your tolerance levels, and the specific stressors that provoke stress reactions in you, are as individual as your tolerance for pain. The next chapter will help you assess your own reactions to life's stressors.

"Faith is the realization of what is hoped for and evidence of things not seen" (Heb 11:1).

---

3 The Difference between Faith and Positive Thinking

"Doc, doc," the suffering patient in the old joke moans. "It hurts when I do that."

"Don't do that," the doctor replies.

If only it could be that simple. It hurts when you worry? So don't worry. Be happy.

Put a driving beat behind that simple message and you've got yourself a hit song (or do, anyway, if you're Bobby McFerrin). But we know it isn't that simple. Don't we? We know, for example, we can't really lose weight without exercise, while eating all and anything we want, simply by taking a pill. Don't we?

They sure seem to sell a lot of those diet pills.

Does positive thinking work?

From Ben Franklin on, Americans have often embraced the notion that a positive mental attitude could call forth a positive reality. Dale Carnegie's *How to Win Friends and Influence People* and Norman Vincent Peale's *The Power of Positive Thinking* have been perennial best-sellers.

In another volume, *Faith Is the Answer*, Peale wrote that the "ultimate method for having faith is simply to have faith." He advised us to eliminate all negative ideas, reduce the "worry words" and empty the mind twice a day, because "fear thoughts, unless drained off, can clog the mind and impede the flow of mental and spiritual power."

But the notion predates Peale and goes back at least to 1916, when Charles Haanel, in his *Master Key System*, described the subconscious mind as a "benevolent stranger, working on your behalf."

"Would you bring into your life more power, get the power consciousness," he advised. "Live the spirit of these things until they become yours by right.... You need not acquire this power. You already have it."

In another hallmark book, *Think and Grow Rich* (1936), Napoleon Hill applied positive thinking to making money. "Riches begin with a state of mind," Hill noted. You must "desire money so keenly that your desire is an obsession." (Perhaps he meant a "state of mine"?)

According to Peale, Hill and others, we create this positive state of mind through autosuggestion. Chant your affirmation often enough, and you will come to believe it. Once you believe it, you will live it.

In 1978, Dr. Joyce Brothers—known to a whole generation of Americans as a TV pitchperson and talk show habitué—repeated this mantra in *How to Get Whatever You Want Out of Life*, teaching us to become "power people." The same year, M. Scott Peck hit the top of the best seller lists with *The Road Less Traveled*—and stayed there for years.

On a more scholarly level, psychologist Abraham Maslow introduced "self-actualization," the process of achieving our full human potential by transcending the ego.

Werner Erhard (born Jack Rosenberg, and a salesman by trade) developed a positive thinking boot camp called

EST, drilling into participants the notion that they have complete control of their lives and no responsibility for anybody else's.

An overweight, broke drifter named Anthony Robbins turned his life around and then told us how to do it too, in books called *Unlimited Power* and *Awaken the Giant Within*, and then in videos and cassettes and television infomercials. Using some of the same positive-thinking principles, Maxie Maultsby Jr. wrote *Help Yourself to Happiness* and founded the International Association for Clear Thinking (ACT).

Books promised to teach us to "have an out-of-body experience in thirty days." Seminar leaders guaranteed to have us walking on burning coals or broken glass in one easy—and expensive—lesson. Computer programs in psychocyberspace promised to eliminate the need for time-consuming mantras or lotus positions with instant mind-alteration.

And Wendy Kaminer decided it was all a bunch of non-sense.

"Americans do penance by buying books that criticize the way they live," she wrote in 1992 in her scathing critique of the self-help movement, *I'm Dysfunctional, You're Dysfunctional* (a book that criticized the way we live). It all boiled down to the "babble of bliss speak," she charged, the eleva-tion of feeling at the expense of rationality, the substitution of "sanctimony for sense."

The self-help hucksters preach simple solutions for complex human problems, she wrote. With no licensing or regulation or accountability in the "self-help industry," she concluded, many followers are the victims of charlatans.

Kaminer surely picked an easy target. Some wolves lurk in the self-help woods, just as there are charlatan evangelists and crooked lawyers and politicians on the take. Things like walking on hot coals surely lends itself to the ridicule of parody.

But we need to be careful before we dismiss the whole notion. Some elements of positive thinking seem to work for some people in some situations. I know a young man who was mired in depression, struggling with self-doubt, on the verge of throwing his life away. He has loving parents and a faith in God that somehow endured even through the darkest times, and these surely sustained him. He also found great help in Tony Robbins' second book. Robbins helped him to affirm himself and to organize his life so that he could cope on the days when he felt like pulling the covers up over his head.

So is Robbins a crook or a savior?

He's likely neither one. Neither was Norman Cousins, the respected editor and writer who after a massive heart attack rehabilitated himself through diet, exercise and that vital component of positive thinking, humor. Laurel and Hardy helped heal him. He wrote about his experience in *The Healing Heart.*

Most of us are familiar with the "placebo effect." When researchers test medications, they give the real thing to half the subjects and a "placebo" (a sugar pill or some equally harmless substance) to the other. The subjects don't know what they're getting, and in a "double blind" test, the dispensers don't know what they're giving, either. Time after time, some of the subjects taking the placebo got well, or at least better.

Did they improve because they believed they were getting effective medicine, and the mere belief made it so? If so, does that mean we can we talk ourselves into a healing mind frame, as Peale and Carnegie and hundreds of others have suggested?

Remember professor Harold Hill? He's the "band

leader" who taught the kids of River City, Iowa to play by the "think system" in Meredith Willson's delightful *Music Man*. If you want to play "Minuet in G," Hill instructed his youthful charges, you must simply *think* "Minuet in G." At the end of the play, Hill, the kids, and romance all triumph as the River City Boys' Band marches down the street, playing not "Minuet in G" but a rousing rendition of "Seventy Six Trombones."

Pure hokum, right? Maybe not.

I've heard numerous anecdotes that indicate that positive thinking can affect something as measurable as athletic performance. One tennis coach in Arizona taped his players in action and created individual highlight tapes. Each player watched himself serve superbly, hit that sizzling backhand passing shot, charge the net, return the lob. From watching the tapes, their play improved significantly.

In one study, researchers had their subjects shoot free throws to establish a baseline level of performance (in English, how many free throws each could make in twenty tries). One third of the subjects then practiced shooting free throws daily. Another third spent their practice time simply visualizing themselves shooting free throws perfectly, swish after swish. The third group didn't do anything, physically or mentally, about free throws.

When the subjects all shot their "post test" free throws, the group that had been diligently shooting free throws every day confirmed the old adage that practice makes, if not perfect, at least better. We would have predicted as much. Predictably, the group that didn't touch or think about a basketball didn't show any improvement.

But we might not have predicted that the group that had been thinking about free throws, without ever actually picking up a ball, also showed improvement, equal to and in some cases greater than the group that had practiced.

I believe in the power of positive visualization. I'll recommend it to you a few chapters ahead, when we talk about public speaking. I know it works; I'm just not sure how.

The difference between thinking and believing

Where does positive thinking leave off and faith begin? Is positive thinking simply faith wearing a secular disguise? If so, faith in what?

Will prayer "work" in the same way that positive thinking seems at times to be effective, calling forth a positive reality from a positive mind set?

In the early 1980s an internist named Dr. Larry Dossey learned of a study that seemed to show that patients in a coronary care unit who were being prayed for every day did better on average than patients not receiving prayers. Neither the nearly 400 patients in the study nor any of the doctors or nurses involved knew who had been assigned to the group getting the prayers.

Dr. Dossey searched through the scientific literature and found more than 100 experiments on the impact of prayer. In more than half of the studies he considered scientifically valid, prayer had a positive effect—on high blood pressure, cancer cells, tumors, even germinating seeds. He wrote about his findings in a book called *Healing Words*.

Is the unseen God answering some of these prayers? If so, why those, and not the others?

Remember the father who brings his son to Jesus to be healed of an unclean spirit? (We'll use the accounts in Matthew 17:14 ff. and in Mark 9:14–29.)

"Lord, have pity on my son, for he...suffers severely; often he falls into fire, and often into water."

The disciples have already failed to cast the spirit out, and the man turns to Jesus in desperation.

"You faithless and perverse generation," Jesus says, "how long will I be with you? How long will I endure you? Bring him here to me."

"If you can do anything," the man pleads in Mark's version of the story, "have compassion on us and help us."

"If you can!" Jesus says. "Everything is possible to one who has faith."

Jesus rebukes the unclean spirit, and it immediately leaves the boy, who is cured.

When the disciples ask why their efforts had failed, Jesus tells them in Matthew's account, "Because of your little faith. Amen, I say to you, if you have faith the size of a mustard seed, you will say to this mountain, 'Move from here to there,' and it will move. Nothing will be impossible for you."

In all three synoptic Gospels, Jesus compares the kingdom of God to a mustard seed, which "...is the smallest of all the seeds on the earth. But once it is sown, it springs up and becomes the largest of plants" (Mk 4:31–32).

Is Jesus really promising us, then, that even a tiny mustard-seed size faith will enable us to move a mountain, or to confidently call on the power of God to heal our sick spirits and minds and bodies?

But how can this be? We have all prayed, from the depths of our faith and our need and our love, for the sickness to pass, for the storm to subside, for the loved one to live. And we have all suffered as our fervent petitions went unfilled. Does that mean our faith just wasn't big enough, not even the size of the mustard seed? Indeed, after my friend Denise died of cancer after having prayed and been prayed over for healing, I heard someone say she would have been healed if her faith had been stronger.

But it isn't like that. Jesus tells us specifically that it isn't, that we can't quantify faith and put it on a scale to see if we have "enough" faith for the various demands we place on God.

Will faith ensure that all our earthly problems will work out according to our wishes? Clearly not. This is where faith differs from positive thinking. Jesus' trust in his Father led him to suffering and death on the cross, despite his entreaty to "let this cup pass." His mother's faith, her willingness to be a handmaiden of the Lord, led her to the foot of her son's cross. Faith and prayer lead us to trust in God, to let go of our desire to control things.

"All things can be done," Jesus assures us, "for the one who believes."

"I believe," the frantic father assures Jesus in Mark's account—but immediately adds "help my unbelief."

He believes—or he wouldn't have come to Jesus with his need in the first place—just as we believe, or we wouldn't pray and participate in Mass and read Scripture. But the father isn't sure he believes enough, isn't sure his faith will be sufficient to merit a healing from Jesus. And neither are we.

> *"All things can be done," Jesus assures us,*
> *"for the one who believes."*
> ———<•>———

From out of our faith ("I believe") we pray for stronger faith ("help my unbelief"). In a way we are affirming Peale's simple tautology that the way to have faith is to have it, or perhaps, to refine it just slightly, the way to have faith is to practice faith, to act always as if we believed in things un- seen, even when we aren't sure we have enough faith.

We do not in fact "have" faith at all, in the sense that we "have" something that can be put in a container and measured and spent and saved, hoarded in the good times and spent in the bad. We live faith. By faith, we know we are the living embodiment of God's love. Faith is a gift from God, who will always give it to us if we ask.

Faith assures us that God is loving and kind, and that his creation is good. Faith gives us certainty that everything will work out according to God's wishes, not our own. In that faith we find our peace and our ability to walk through the dark valley without fear.

"Can any of you by worrying add a single hour to your span of life?" (Mt 6:27).

---

4 Time Management Didn't Save Us—How Faith Can Heal Speed Sickness

We keep building more roads and raising the speed limits, but we wind up stuck in traffic anyway—and it's driving us crazy. In Seattle a few years ago, a motorist blocked by traffic could stand it no more. She drove her car onto the sidewalk and ran over a pedestrian.

We worship speed. We struggle to save time, buy time, gain time. We hate wasting time, killing time, and serving time. Our labor-saving devices were supposed to give us more time. But instead of being liberated, we spend our time buying, maintaining, worrying about and repairing our gadgets and making enough money to afford more of them, while time to play and pray vanishes.

Our fax machines, e-mail and voice mail were supposed to help us get our work done faster. But we don't work shorter; we've simply increased our expectations of how much we should be able to do in a day, working longer and longer while slipping further and further behind.

In the late 1800s, the sixty-hour work week was the

norm. By 1910, that figure had dropped to fifty-one hours, and in 1929, as the stock market got ready to take its famous swan dive, the average American was putting in forty-four hours per week between punch in and punch out. We bottomed out at about thirty-nine hours a week in the early 1970s, and sociologists were announcing the arrival of the Age of Leisure.

But a funny thing happened on our way to the perpetual vacation. We stopped working shorter and started working longer again. Now the average worker puts in about 164 extra hours of paid labor—that's an extra month of work— each year. And after working killingly long hours and enduring our hectic schedules, we bring more work home with us. No wonder so many of us resent our jobs and ruin God's day dreading Monday.

Even when we seek a little fun and relaxation, we don't stop speeding. We perch in front of our VCRs, remote controls clutched in our fists as we fast forward through the slow spots, zap the commercials, graze from station to station. If the story doesn't grab us—right now—we flee to another. Entertain us, we demand—and be quick about it.

News has become just another entertainment, another hurry-up symptom of our speed sickness. Television news programs offer vivid images of the daily disasters and reduce every significant utterance to a seven-second "sound bite." Newspapers and magazines break stories into briefs, sidebars and digests.

The violent rhythms of football have replaced the gentler unfolding of baseball as our national game, while our lives have become a series of two-minute drills.

We eat so fast that we hardly notice what we're eating. By the time our stomachs can get the signal back to our mouths to cease stuffing, we've consumed well beyond need or even satiation.

Relatively few of us read books. Books are too slow, and they're too much work. We have easier ways to get information and to have our stories told to us. Nature itself has become too slow for us, so we capture and compress it with time-lapse photography. Perhaps we're so quick to destroy our earth because we no longer take the time to experience it.

Mismanaging time

Enter time management to save us from ourselves.

Books purporting to tell us how to live more time-efficient lives date back at least to 1910 and Arnold Bennett's *How to Live on 24 Hours a Day.* But the time management movement began in earnest in 1973—about the time the work week was reversing direction and starting to lengthen —when Alan Lakein gave the movement its classic text, *How to Get Control of Your Time and Your Life.*

You must "work smarter, not harder," Lakein told us. You need to exert control over your time, make a daily to-do list, establish A, B and C priorities, rank the A items, and tackle all the A-1 essential items before going on to the A-2s.

Use commute, coffee break, lunch and waiting times productively, Lakein said. Don't sleep your life away. Handle paper once. Screen out the irrelevant. Say "no" to the time-wasters. Above all, constantly ask yourself "Lakein's question"—"What's the best use of my time right now?"

Lakein warned against becoming a compulsive overorganizer, an overdoer, a "time nut." He advised us to allow for flexibility by scheduling free time. Relaxing, he maintained, is a good use of time, and sometimes you can get more done by doing nothing.

But many ignored this wisdom. New gurus of the Clock

Racer Movement rushed their own versions of it into print, without the warnings about becoming obsessive.

A few, like Tony and Robbie Fanning in their book *Get It All Done and Still Be Human*, set as the goal feeling good rather than doing more. A few, like Steven Covey in *The 7 Habits of Highly Effective People*, based life management on personal values. But most of the time management books and tapes that followed Lakein stressed packing every minute of every day with as much "useful" activity as possible.

"Experts" advised us to become "polychronic" by learning to do two, three, four, five things at once. Workshops promised to help us manage "multiple projects, objectives and deadlines." We were told to emulate champions of polychronisity (sorry) like talk show host Joan Rivers, who had a speakerphone on her treadmill.

A speakerphone on her treadmill?

We learned to work time to death. We didn't live; we scheduled. Instead of listening to the inner voice, we heard the ticking of the clock. We weren't living in the moment. We were living in the next one, constantly seeking a horizon that kept receding no matter how fast we ran to reach it. We wound up feeling wrung out, strung out and stressed out. What we didn't feel was good.

At the end of another frantic day, when it should have been time at last to lay our burdens down, we even shaved time from sleep, so that eighty percent of us, according to some estimates, are now chronically sleep-deprived.

"The rush and the pressure of modern life are a form, perhaps the most common form, of its innate violence," Thomas Merton wrote. "To allow oneself to be carried away by a multitude of conflicting concerns, to surrender to many demands, to commit oneself to many projects, to want to help in everything, is to succumb to violence."

Getting back to fundamental principles

Remember when the disciples were accused of violating the sabbath because they had paused in a field to pluck off heads of grain to eat?

"The sabbath was made for man," Jesus told them, "not man for the sabbath" (Mk 2:27).

God didn't create the sabbath to hurt us. He didn't give us the ability to create clocks and computers so we could torture ourselves; he gave us good gifts to help us. God didn't give us time to manage; he gave us life to live. He didn't create us as slaves; he made us his sons and daughters.

God lets you decide how you will live. You get to choose how much is enough and how good is good enough. You get to decide what's a "waste of time" and what isn't. If you make a schedule, you get to decide when to follow and when to abandon the schedule you made.

God didn't give us time to manage;
he gave us life to live.

———<◆>———

Stay loose, flexible, open to the moment. Know that the most important thing you'll do today may not be on your to-do list.

God gave me a clear lesson about this when I was in the midst of my study of time management and had just learned the techniques for getting rid of the "time wasters" (people with either less to do or a more leisurely sense of how long they have to get it done).

I was very busy. Oh, I was *always* very busy, much too

busy for interruptions. One day a friend and former colleague appeared at my office door. He had always been a chatter, a storyteller, a slow talker. Newly retired, he had lots of time for visiting.

Not with *me*, he didn't. I would manage him so smoothly, he'd never even know what hit him.

I stood up; that's the first rule. I moved toward the door; that's rule number two. Don't let them invade your territory, and whatever you do, don't let them sit down. Bodies in motion tend to remain in motion, physics tells us, while bodies at rest tend to sit in the chair, sipping coffee and gabbing, while precious time ticks away. I prepared to sweep my friend right back out the door.

"Don't do it."

Was it really a voice in my mind, or do I only imagine so now, in the retelling?

"Let him stay."

Whatever the source, the message was quite clear, and for once, I obeyed the inner voice. I backed off, offering him a chair (while the familiar voice in my mind shrieked "No! No! Don't do it! We're doomed!").

He gently closed the door behind him and came straight to the point. He had cancer and needed an operation the following week. He had told the family but not any of his other former colleagues. He was telling me because he considered me his friend.

He was very scared.

I didn't have words to take away his pain. But I cared and told him so, told him I would pray for him. I even gripped one of his hands in mine as he cried a little. In a few minutes, he stood, heaved a sigh, thanked me and left. He seemed to feel better for having been able to share his burden, if only for a moment. I knew then—and I know it even more now—

that my short conversation with a former colleague that day was the most important, the most human thing I accomplished all day. And it wasn't even on my to-do list.

The phone rang. I was still feeling shaky so I let it ring. Does that sound like heresy? You really *can* let a phone ring. I didn't know that for the longest time. It's okay to postpone a phone conversation until you're ready to have it. That's what answering machines are for.

We get to decide.

We get to decide whether or not to open the mail, respond to the fax, read the magazine, turn on the television, pay any attention to it once it's on, or throw it in the garbage.

We're supposed to use the tools, not let them run us.

The most important thing you'll do today may not be on your to-do list.

———⟨◆⟩———

I'm learning to identify and separate the vital from the merely urgent. Getting to the airport on time is urgent. Nourishing my relationship with God is vital. If I live only in the apparent crisis of the moment, I never have time for the truly important things of life, and my spirit withers for lack of nourishment.

I'm learning to give myself enough lead time to do the job right and still enjoy my life. I'm learning not to time that dash downtown so that I have to hit every traffic light and find a parking place right in front of the building to be on time for my appointment. I leave early. If I get stuck in traffic, I welcome the wait as an opportunity to breathe deeply and pray.

Time managers tell us that over a lifetime the average American will spend seven years in the bathroom, six years eating, five years waiting in line, three years sitting in meetings (but it will seem like thirty-three), two years playing telephone tag, eight months opening junk mail, and six months sitting at red lights. Don't get frustrated. Turn the wait time into rest time and prayer time.

Can't "find the time" to pray? That's because it isn't lost. We must make the time. If necessary, schedule three or four "prayer breaks" in the midst of even the busiest day. (Make that *especially* the busiest day.) Read a passage from Scripture. Then close your eyes, letting your racing heart slow down. Feel God's presence in your very breath.

I spent a very long time learning to do two, three and four things at a time. Now I'm rediscovering the grace of doing one thing, the most important thing, well. Whatever that one thing is, even the most menial task, I do it in accordance with my first principle, my reason for living.

What's your purpose in life? What is that "one thing only" that Jesus told Martha to be mindful of? Isn't it to love and serve the Lord, right here, right now?

When asked to name the greatest commandment in the Torah, Jesus told us to "love the Lord your God with all your heart, with all your soul, with all your mind, and with all your strength" and to "love your neighbor as yourself. There is no other commandment greater than these" (Mk 12:30–31).

With these simple words as the basis for everything you do, you can change almost anything about the way you live each day. You can catch yourself before you act, replacing the old time-centered response with the new God-centered one. The more often you succeed, the easier it will be to believe in the next success. Take note of and enjoy all your triumphs, no matter how small.

Anything of real worth or importance takes time. You may have fallen in love at first glance, but building a relationship takes a lifetime. The impulse to lose forty pounds, write a novel, or climb a mountain may come in an instant. But crash diets don't work, there are no "crash novels," and there's no short way up the mountain. Carrying out your intention and your commitment takes a lifetime.

"When I was young I thought that we climbed a mountain to reach a plateau," the poet Donald Hall wrote. "Now I know that we climb to climb.... The work is the thing and not the response to the work.... So what if it takes us a long time to write a poem?" he concluded. "What are we living for anyway?"

"Do not be afraid any longer, little flock, for your Father is pleased to give you the kingdom" (Lk 12:32).

---

5   Don't Sweat the Small Stuff

Writing a novel is like driving at night, author E. L. Doctorow once said. You can only see a little way ahead, but you can follow your headlights all the way to your destination.

Most of us like to know where we're going. We study guidebooks and plot our course on a map. We get our cars tuned before we leave and phone ahead for motel reservations, so we know we'll have a comfortable and safe resting place.

But no matter how much we prepare and how carefully we plan, we must at last submit to the unknown road. We can only drive the stretch of road we're on right now, with all its surprises. Such is the wisdom the road imparts. Life is the journey, not the destination.

Some of those surprises will be wonderful—unexpected beauty around the next bend in the road, chance encounters with remarkable people, fluffy biscuits and fresh orange juice in a rundown roadside diner.

"One day at a time," Alcoholics Anonymous advises in the original twelve-step recovery program that has helped countless people control their addictions. You don't try to stop drinking forever. You don't think about a lifetime without another drink. You simply don't drink today, now. Tomorrow you get up and do it again. When you do, God will be there to greet you in the sunrise.

"The favors of the Lord are not exhausted, his mercies are not spent; they are renewed each morning, so great is his faithfulness" (Lam 3:22–23).

Life is the journey, not the destination.

———⟨◆⟩———

Jesus taught us not to worry about tomorrow, which will surely have worries of its own. He said we should ask our Father for *today's* bread, not for a warehouse full of bread to last us a lifetime. When poor Martha got too busy with her chores to sit and listen, Jesus gently chided her to take advantage of the precious moment, the sacred now.

Only one thing is required: that we love God *now*, this moment. We must live and love in the present tense.

Separating the small stuff from the big stuff

"Don't sweat the small stuff," folk wisdom advises.

Isn't life mostly made up of small stuff?

Years ago, Willie Davis, then a graceful centerfielder for the Los Angeles Dodgers, established an unwanted World Series record by committing three errors in one inning, helping the Baltimore Orioles to victory. That had to hurt.

When the great Dodger announcer, Vin Scully, came to the clubhouse to interview Davis after the game, he found a man at peace with himself.

"It ain't my life," Davis told Scully, "and it ain't my wife. So why worry?"

His life wasn't at stake. His relationship with his life's mate wasn't in jeopardy. He couldn't change what had already happened. So even his performance in the most intense competition his profession offers was small stuff, not worthy of sweat.

That's not to say Davis didn't care. He just didn't *worry*. Caring for a professional athlete means conditioning mind and body, honing skills through endless practice, and remaining fully alert while on the field. Worrying means stewing about things you did but wished you hadn't or things you must do but are afraid you can't. Caring helps; worry hurts.

Okay. So we shouldn't sweat the small stuff, even "small stuff" like muffing two fly balls and overthrowing a base in a World Series game. But what about the REALLY big stuff, like the health and well-being of your family, or your quest to discern God's will for you?

Writing your "Worryography"

Spend a few minutes on a reflection that will help you put the big worries in proper perspective. You'll need a special "worry journal" for this reflection and the ones that follow in this book. Don't just read the directions. DO it!

What was your biggest worry when you were five years old? Write it down on the first page of your journal. What were you most anxious about in high school? At the top of page two, write that one down, too. On page three, write down your biggest worry from ten years ago.

Now go back to the first page and revisit that childhood worry. What form did the worry take? Did you tell anyone? If so, what words did you use? What other feelings came with the worry? Write your answers.

Now write down the outcome. How did the problem get resolved? Did you solve the problem? Perhaps you simply outgrew the condition. Are you still worried now about what you were worried about then?

Now do the same for that high school anxiety and the decade-old devilment. Do you see any pattern in the types of things you worried about, the words you use to describe them, and the feelings you associate with your worries? What constants do you find in your "worry history"? Recognizing them in past worries will help you identify, name and conquer present and future anxieties.

Now the big question. For each of the life situations or conditions you just wrote about, what part did worry play in the outcome? Specifically, *did worrying help you in any way?*

I didn't think so. It never helps me, either. So, why are we worrying?

What's your biggest worry right now? Search carefully for the words and write them down on the fourth page of your worry journal. Be as specific as you can. Again, what other feelings do you associate with the worry?

Will worrying about the problem or condition help in any way? No? Then let the worry go. Give the problem to God in prayer. Ask him to help you deal with it.

All of our worries fall into one of two categories: small stuff, not really worth sweating, and big stuff, which all the sweat in the world won't help. So let's turn all our stuff, big and little, over to God, who sweats it all for us.

On the fifth page of your worry journal, copy this quotation:

"Are not two sparrows sold for a small coin? Yet not one of them falls to the ground without your Father's knowledge.... So do not be afraid; you are worth more than many sparrows" (Mt 10:29, 31).

Jesus is talking to you. Talk back. Write out your response to this beautiful promise.

Come back to this passage often. It's awfully hard to worry while you're in the presence of such a loving God.

"For human beings it is impossible, but not for God. All things are possible for God" (Mk 10:27).

---

6 Continuing the Faith Journey and the Worry Journal

You can no more save yourself from worry than you can save yourself from death. But God can do it—if you let him.

Bring that heart full of anxiety to your loving God. It's hard, isn't it? We're all so accustomed to pretending, hiding our fears from a critical world. You're not supposed to talk about your fear that your husband is falling out of love with you or that your teenager doesn't respect you or that you're developing a double chin or that the next pink slip at the office might have your name on it.

Our society views such worries as a sign of weakness, an indication that you're not in control of your life. We go right on having the worries, of course. But we add layers of denial, judgment and guilt.

Whoa. Back up. Who said you were supposed to be in control of your life? You're not, you know. Yes, you have free will. You decide if, when and whom to marry and how many children to have and where to live and whether to have the double bacon cheeseburger or the garden salad with low-fat dressing.

But you didn't create the world, you didn't earn entry

into it, and you don't know for sure what's around the next corner, much less eternity.

Set aside guilt and judgment. If you're a worrier, you're God's worrier. Stop denying. Face your anxiety squarely. Respect and honor your feelings, including the "unacceptable" ones, like anxiety, envy, hatred....

God didn't command us to love our neighbor because we were naturally going to do it anyway. Being human, we feel all sorts of things that aren't anything like love. We're commanded not to feel love but to love, to treat others as we want others to treat us, with consideration and concern.

Catching yourself in the act

To accept and deal with your worry, you first have to catch yourself worrying. That doesn't sound hard—your awareness of and dissatisfaction with your worrying led you to this book, after all. But if like me you've made a career of trying to be perfect (and thus, not subject to anxiety), you've probably gotten good at hiding your worries, even from yourself.

The worry's there, all right. But it may have gone underground, into the subconscious—to surface in bad dreams and late night "formless furies," and in physical symptoms ranging from muscle spasms and headaches to high blood pressure and heart disease.

Turn to the fifth page in your worry journal. You'll be writing just for you; no one ever has to see the worries you reveal here. Several times a day if you can, and at least once at the end of each day, take a few minutes to take stock of your worries and your feelings.

Date your entry. Note the time of day and where you are. Write your worries out as specifically as you can, in as much detail as possible. Give the worries substance. Push beneath the surface. The apparent cause of your concern may be masking a deeper, more fundamental fear. (Yes, you're worried about the report due Friday, but underneath that specific worry, maybe you really doubt your competence to perform your job.)

How will you find time to keep a worry journal every day? You won't find time. No one will give it to you, either. If you're really committed to letting God heal your anxieties, you'll *make* time. Schedule these sessions. Write them down on the to-do list and in the day-planner if that's what it takes. Write this appointment in ink and make sure you keep it.

Pray that your session will lead you to the awareness you seek and the healing you need. You might begin with a bit of encouragement from the psalms, one of the praise psalms, perhaps (147–150 are great), or this pep talk from Psalm 118:6:

"The Lord is with me; I am not afraid; what can mortals do against me?" (Ps 118:6).

Write freely. Don't evaluate. Don't judge. Don't edit. Don't censor. Just keep pen or pencil moving. It doesn't have to be literature. It just has to be yours, and it has to be true.

As you write, your true fears may emerge from the shadows. Acknowledge them. You may or may not be able to trace the fear back to some specific experience in the past. What matters is that you recognize and face the fear now. Open yourself to your feelings, own them, embrace them as a part of who you are.

You don't have to come up with a "solution." You're simply identifying, exploring and experiencing your fears, just as they are. That's enough work for now.

Stick with your worry journal for at least three weeks before deciding whether the technique is doing you any good. You may feel uncomfortable or even foolish at first, and you may be unable to penetrate the wall of denial you've built around your worry. Don't abandon the quest.

As you begin to give shape to your anxieties, you may find that some of them vanish. Many fears are spawned in darkness. When you expose them to the light, they evaporate.

Talk back to the worries that remain. Are things *really* that bad, or are you being unrealistic? We dismiss optimism as "wishful thinking" and elevate pessimism as "realistic." This is nonsense. Pessimism and optimism are mindsets. They become habitual. Expectations of success are no less realistic than forebodings of doom.

> *Many fears are spawned in darkness.*
> *When you expose them to the light, they evaporate.*

――――――<◆>――――――

You may have negative self-evaluations yammering at you just beneath consciousness. Bring them to the surface and write them down.

"I'm socially inept, a real nerd," the inner voice hisses.

Write the words at the top of a page in your worry journal. Then write sentences exaggerating your fear:

"I have THREE left feet."

"I can't chew gum and think at the same time."

"Pigs at the trough have better manners than I do."

Then talk back to the original statement:

"Actually, I'm as presentable as the next person."

"No one has ever seemed offended or even mildly put off by anything I've said or done."

Relax. Lighten up. Talk back some more. Have some fun.

"I never butter my bread with my thumb."

"Burping used to be taken as a compliment for the chef."

End your session by noting an appropriate Scripture passage, such as:

"I sought the Lord, who answered me, [and] delivered me from all my fears" (Ps 34:5).

"My heart pounds within me; death's terrors fall upon me.... But I will call upon God, and the Lord will save me" (Ps 55:5, 17).

Next time you feel the anxiety emerging, call forth some of the statements you wrote and the Scripture passage you cited to combat it. Repeat as often as necessary.

Play the "what are the odds?" game with your fears. Realistically, what is the likelihood of your worst fears being realized? What does experience teach you? Have you confronted a similar fear in the past? If so, how was it resolved?

If the *worst* does come to pass, will you be able to deal with it? Underlying much of your worry may be the implicit notion that you're incapable of handling the situation. Talk back to that foolish notion, too. You've handled lots of challenges. You can also handle the next one.

Will your worry journal clear up all your anxieties? No. Worries will remain. But you will have dispelled some of them and gained awareness and insight into how your thoughts and feelings interact. You'll have begun to develop valuable skills for your journey out of anxiety and toward trust.

Let God guide you every step of this journey. Let God's Word provide direction and comfort.

"When I say, 'my foot is slipping,' your love, Lord, holds me up. When cares increase within me, your comfort gives me joy" (Ps 94:18–19).

On the night before he died, Jesus prayed in the garden that he might not have to drink from the cup of death. God didn't remove the cup, but he did ease the anxiety, enabling Jesus to face his trial.

Our loving God will do no less for you.

"There is an appointed time for everything, and a time for every affair under the heavens" (Eccl 3:1).

---

7   Meeting Worry Head On

You've begun to identify and talk back to your anxieties. Now you'll begin to break their power over you and turn them into a prayer of thanksgiving.

Get out your calendar and schedule worry time. Write the appointment down, but don't plan on going beyond ten minutes. You can start or end your day with worry or use the appointment as a tension reliever in the midst of a busy day. Your worry journal may have already shown you your peak "worry times." Consider scheduling your worry break for a time when you're naturally anxious. When I'm on the road, I generally find myself flooded with anxiety right around sunset. So sundown on the highway is an excellent time for my worry break.

Whatever time you select, be sure you keep your appointment. If a family emergency arises, you'll of course tend to that instead (and reschedule your worry date). But if the "emergency" wouldn't keep you from a business meeting or a social engagement, it mustn't keep you from your worry appointment either. Respect your worry time as fully as anything else on the calendar.

Suppose you schedule a worry break for Monday morning, right after the kids leave for school. You're going to honor that date, but of course your worry won't. Worry doesn't wait. It will catch you while you're resting on Saturday afternoon and pounce. When it does, simply send it away.

Tell the worry, "Not now. I've got you scheduled for Monday morning."

The worry will come storming back on Sunday night. Don't get mad at yourself, and don't panic. Just tell the worry to go away. Keep telling it every time it returns.

The worry will get more subtle, seeping into subconscious thought and even into dreams. When you catch yourself "entertaining" that worry, don't chide yourself, and don't despair. Just send it away again.

It takes practice. You've been building the worry habit for a long time, so long that it has become an automatic part of your thought process. Be patient and forgiving with yourself. Turn to Scripture for guidance and comfort. Try Philippians 4:6–7, which tells us:

"Do not worry about anything, but in everything by prayer and supplication with thanksgiving let your requests be made known to God. And the peace of God, which surpasses all understanding, will guard your hearts and your minds in Christ Jesus."

As you become successful at scheduling your worries, you'll be able to enjoy the rest of life more fully, focusing your energies on work and worship, relationship and recreation, rather than on worry. You'll be fully present to loved ones, friends and colleagues. That's the power of focused living in the moment.

When you banish your anxiety between worry sessions, your subconscious mind has a chance to ponder causes and solutions. We don't really understand how this incredible gift of God works. We don't even agree on what to call it ("right side of the brain," "muse," "voice of the spirit").

Perhaps Charles Haanel came closest, way back in 1916, when he called the subconscious a "benevolent stranger, working on your behalf."

Understand it or not, the subconscious constantly plays with images and ideas, with total disregard for natural, moral and ethical law. That explains why you can have a dream you don't approve of or even understand. The subconscious breaks all the rules that govern the waking mind. You can't control this process, but you can give it time to happen, and you can pay attention to its rich yield.

Facing down the monster

Worry time is here at last. The kids are off at school. You've unplugged the phone and done your best to eliminate other potential distractions.

Now, just how do you keep a worry appointment? Should you have a special "worry" place, with just the right atmosphere for worry? Would music help or hurt? (What's the best music to worry by?) What's the proper "worry" position—sitting, standing, lying on a couch?

None of this matters. Get comfortable, so that your body won't interrupt you. Remove yourself from anything that might distract you.

Scared? Any step into the unknown is frightening. Amy Tan, author of *The Joy Luck Club*, writes of being chased by her fear. She learned to stop running, turn and face the monster, even while every instinct in her screamed to keep running.

You've stopped running at last. Now what? What exactly are you supposed to *do?* Just let the worry happen. Experience it—*all* of it. That's "all" you have to do.

Doing this kind of "nothing" may be one of the toughest tasks you ever do. Open yourself to the full force. Feel it all.

Flooding with your worry can feel like an inner earthquake or a spiraling descent into a dark pit. Christ is with you. Nothing bad will happen to you. The feelings can't really hurt you; only the constant strain of fighting them off can hurt.

Let fear run its course. The storm will subside, replaced by a peace much deeper than the mere absence of fear. You've survived the worst! You've embraced the monster. And it didn't kill you! Truth to tell, it didn't even hurt.

Let fear run its course. The storm will subside,
replaced by a peace much deeper than
the mere absence of fear.

———<♦>———

"Silly me, to have been so scared of being scared," you think. But you weren't being silly; you were being human. We're all afraid to be afraid.

Thank God for being with you in your worry and for seeing you through safely. Thank God for the worry itself. Yes! The worry is a part of the life God has given you, part of the energy and force that make you who you are. Embrace it all. Then get on with your life. The worry will return, but it will have been humbled by its failure to shake you loose from your faith.

What if you show up for your worry appointment and your worry doesn't?

No monster appears, no hurricane envelops you. Perhaps you can't relax your lifelong guard against letting yourself experience your anxiety. That's not surprising, is it? After all these years of evading, you can't expect to face your fears in a day.

Use your worry time to pray. Make another appointment. Go back to your day-to-day activities.

Now the worry shows up! It wasn't gone, after all, just late. Send it away. Let tension and frustration build for your next appointment.

When you and your worry meet again, your loving God will be with you, guiding you through the darkness of worry and into the light of peace.

Jesus asked him, "What is your name?" He replied, "Legion is my name. There are many of us" (Mk 5:9).

---

8 Moving from Feeling to Doing

Some folks use alcohol or other drugs to relieve anxiety. Some escape into television, sex, romance novels, video games—anything to keep from feeling and confronting their pain.

The drug of choice in our culture is overactivity. We carry our day-planners everywhere. We create to-do lists that never get done. Got a blank spot on the calendar? Plug it. Keep moving. If you aren't exhausted at the end of the day, you aren't doing your fair share.

We'll never confront the pain until we stop running. We'll never embrace true freedom in the love of God if we rely on all our painkillers. Admit you're hooked. Shun the drug. Let your anxiety flood you.

Sometimes that's all you need to do. But for more persistent and subtle anxieties, you need to determine the specific cause. I often discover the source of my anxiety by confronting myself with mental images and letting my emotional "Geiger counter" (for me a fluttering in my chest or a burning in the stomach) tell me when I've found the anxiety provoker.

Once you recognize the source of your fear, turn it over to God in prayer. Pray as Jesus did in the garden: "Your will, not mine, be done."

With God's guidance, determine whether you can do anything about the cause of your anxiety. Don't evade. Act in the face of your fear, knowing that God is with you in your struggle. Only when you act in the face of your fear can you grow in wisdom and self-assurance.

> *Once you recognize the source of your fear, turn it over to God in prayer.*

————‹◆›————

If there's nothing to be done, do nothing. Experience and identify the anxiety and move on.

"But I've always been a worrier," you say. "It's just the way I am." I understand. I've always been a worrier, too. But we learn to worry, learn to expect the worst, learn to think that we are incompetent to deal with life. We can learn to replace worry with action and to expect positive results.

Acknowledge your fear as a sign that you're fully alive. Use its energy to empower you to act. You can transform worry into anticipation, fear into excitement.

Next time the anxiety erupts, review these six steps for turning anxiety into energy:

Step one: don't resist or deny the fear.

You'll only send it underground, where it will fester and resurface, stronger than ever, to attack when you're most vulnerable. Face your fear. Let it wash through you. Feel all of it. As you stop fearing the fear, the panic will subside. Worry will have done its worst.

Step two: give form to the fear.

Sometimes fear comes disguised as the formless furies, vague dread or anxiety that can shake you out of a sound sleep and leave you wide-awake until daybreak. Or it may take on a specific but false aspect. Track your fear to its true source. Give it a name. If it helps, write the worry down, as specifically as you can.

Sometimes, merely bringing the fear out of darkness and into the light will cause it to vanish. If not, having named it, you can begin to deal with your fear effectively.

Step three: push the fear to the ultimate.

The fear doesn't exist apart from you. It's a reaction that takes place inside you. Since you created it, you can use it, rechannel it or diffuse it.

Ask yourself two questions: *What's the worst that can happen—really? What are the odds that the worst will happen?*

If that doesn't dissipate the fear, move on to the next step.

Step four: figure out what, if anything, you can do.

Brainstorm your options (including the option to do nothing). Play with the possibilities. Submit your decision to prayer and choose the option that seems best. If you wrote down the problem, write your decision down, too.

When the worry comes back, gently remind yourself, *"I've already decided about that."*

You may be wasting a lot of time worrying about decisions you can't make yet. If so, tell yourself *"I don't have to decide that now."* Say it as often as you need to. Write down the time when and place where you will decide. Let your subconscious play with the worry.

Tell yourself, *"Whatever I decide will be fine."* Say it often enough and you'll begin to believe it, not because you've brainwashed yourself but because the Spirit in you will guide you to the truth of the statement.

Step five: act in spite of the fear.

You feel your inner fears, but you see the composed masks of others, so you might figure nobody else worries. T'ain't so. They can't see your fears, either, so they probably figure you're cool and calm unless you choose to tell them otherwise.

Courage isn't lack of fear. Courage is acting despite and through your fear, rechanneling that fear into energy and alertness. Don't pretend you're not afraid. Experience your fear fully. As it runs its course, gentle calm will replace it.

Often you must act before you feel confident to act. Take several deep, cleansing breaths. Expect to be successful. Then act as if you're no longer afraid.

Step six: abide in your decision.

Make each decision only once. Whatever you do, do it wholeheartedly and then get on with your life.

Time to stop running. Time to breathe deeply. Look around. Pray. Listen. When we break the momentum, anxiety no longer runs us, no longer robs us of our joy, of the quiet goodness of living, of a rich appreciation of God's creation and our place in that creation.

If we fill every moment with evasions, we leave no room for Spirit, no chance to hear God's will: God speaks in the still small voice, but the tornado of activity drowns it out.

You won't eliminate all worry; you wouldn't want to. But you will seek out and confront your anxieties. When you do, you'll be able to respond to life's challenges, and you'll be free to live a spirit-filled life.

If you worry about tomorrow—a phantom that exists only in your mind—you fail to live today, which is rich and real, all you have and all you'll ever need.

You don't need tomorrow to make you whole or to give your life meaning. You are whole in this moment. You have everything you need here and now; you can teach yourself everything you need to know. This isn't wishful thinking. This is the fundamental truth of your existence. You have only to claim it.

<❖>

Six steps for turning anxiety into energy:

1. Don't resist or deny the fear.

2. Give form to the fear.

3. Push the fear to the ultimate.

4. Figure out what, if anything, you can do.

5. Act in spite of the fear.

6. Abide in your decision.

<❖>

"I came so that they might have life and have it more abundantly" (Jn 10:10).

9 How the Prayer Card Can Defeat Five Kinds of Worry

Jesus faced down the devil in the desert, and he called out the demons by name. Like the Master, we need to know the enemy and to call it by name. Here are five common varieties of worry:

1) Anxiety thriving on ignorance

"A little knowledge is a dangerous thing," the poet Alexander Pope noted.

We read a lot about disease and its prevention these days. A bulletin warns that a certain food causes cancer (at least in those poor, long-suffering lab rats). Another bulletin announces that a different food prevents cancer, or at least improves our odds of avoiding it. Next week, new studies come out, and the foods switch places.

In the 1950s, conscientious mothers served their children a hearty, balanced breakfast of bacon and eggs, or maybe pancakes with syrup and butter, with a big glass of whole milk on the side. Now some would call such a mother an assassin, and we're advised to strap on the old nose bag and eat as many oats as we can hold.

The barrage of information and misinformation can be awfully confusing, and it can also provoke a lot of anxiety about what we eat.

2) Worry lurking in the future

Next week you're scheduled to speak before a group of strangers in a distant city. It sounded like a wonderful opportunity when you made the commitment seven months ago. But the closer you get to the day, the more anxious you feel.

You're worried about getting to the airport, worried about catching the plane and making that crucial connecting flight, worried about getting your exercise and eating properly on the road, worried about your family while you're gone, worried about the work that will pile up in your absence....

You're worried, in short, about lots of things you can't do anything about yet. The trip is next week, but the anxiety is building right now.

3) Worry festering in the past

You're sure your friend took your remark the wrong way. You're worried you may have hurt her feelings, extended a misunderstanding, damaged or even destroyed a friendship.

You can apologize and explain, but that may simply fan the flames. (Besides, deep down, you don't *really* think it was your fault.) Even if you do apologize, you can never unsay your hurting remark; your friend may be able to forgive but not forget. So worry lingers, a weight on your heart.

4) Worry feeding on inertia

Resealing the driveway is a messy, difficult job. You hate it, and so you've put it off all summer (it's too hot, too humid, too perfect) and most of the fall. Now you wake up in the middle of the night, worrying that you've waited too long. It's too late now, that middle-of-the-night voice hisses. By next spring, your driveway will be a strip of asphalt shards, and you'll have to replace it.

5) Worry thriving on evasion

If you take that new job in a distant city, you'll be throwing away everything you've worked so hard for—including a handsome retirement package. You'll also be forsaking your friends, yanking the kids out of school, and leaving a nurturing home, neighborhood and parish.

But the new job offers stimulation, challenge, and a good chance for advancement. You've visited the area and like it very much. Truth to tell, that good, secure job with the retirement plan has become unsatisfying, and you really can't see it leading to any new challenges.

You put all the reasons to move on one side, all the reasons to stay on the other, and the scale balances evenly. Each choice carries big potential benefits. Each carries a big price tag. You don't want to pay, and so you put off making any decision. But you go right on worrying.

Making your prayer card

"Come to me, all you who labor and are burdened, and I will give you rest" (Mt 11:28).

Five different kinds of worry call for five different approaches. But in each case, the process begins with letting the Lord in with you.

Take a 3 x 5 (or, if you're a big worrier like me, a 6 x 9) card. On one side, write down the problem that has your head and heart in knots. As with the worry journal, be as specific as you can. The better you define the problem, the better you can deal with it.

On the back of the card, write down a possible solution or solutions. Let your mind roam, and write down anything that comes to you, no matter how apparently silly or impractical. When you're sure you're finished, wait a moment, pencil or pen in hand, your mind as quiet as you can make it, and wait to see if anything else comes.

Now, card in hand, enter into God's presence. Close your eyes and imagine Jesus before you. In times of stress and heartache, I visualize the Good Shepherd, staff in hand, eyes alert and compassionate, watching over me. My heart quiets. The chattering in my head stills. I begin to know that with Jesus I can handle any problem.

Tell him your problem, then listen for an answer. On the prayer card, underneath the problem write down what you feel you should do about it. Then write down *when you intend to do it.* Not "sometime" or "later" or even "next week." Choose a specific day and time.

With Jesus I can handle any problem.

———<◆>———

Different kinds of worry may lead you toward different solutions.

1) Worry thriving on ignorance

We started with a line from Alexander Pope: "A little knowledge is a dangerous thing." The second line provides our solution for worry thriving on ignorance: "Drink deeply," Pope advised, "or taste not of the Pierian Spring" of knowledge.

Suppose that you're worried that your diet is not healthful and would like to change it. Take the time to find out what you need to know. Proper diet is worth more than a glance at the morning paper or half an ear cocked at the radio or television. Newspapers like *The New York Times* and magazines like *American Health Magazine* and *Health* publish material in plain, simple English on the latest research findings and their implications. Specialty magazines like *Countdown*, the magazine of the Juvenile Diabetes Foundation, provide more detail.

Should we believe everything we see in print? Of course not. Does that mean we shouldn't read any of it? Quite the contrary. Thorough study can help us make sound decisions about what we eat and drink—and other aspects of our lives—and can relieve us of the anxiety that stems from ignorance.

After you've studied and prayed and listened for God's guidance, write on your prayer card exactly what changes in diet you intend to make. Then stop worrying and start doing.

2) *Worry lurking in the future*

What can you do about that presentation you have to make in a distant city? Arrange for flights with sufficient time between them. Prepare, check and rehearse your presentation. Arrange accommodations at a facility that includes an exercise room. Get as much work done ahead of time as possible, and arrange to have important contingencies covered while you're gone. Ask a friend to check in with your family to make sure all is well.

Write down on your prayer card all the preparations you intend to make and then do them.

3) *Worry festering in the past*

Have you really done all you can to ease your friend's hurt? Can you let go of your concern about who's right and who's wrong and simply apologize in Christian humility? If so, write the words you'll use on your card. Then write down the time and place where you intend to say them.

What if you decide there's nothing you can really do to make things better? On your card, write in big, bold letters: "THERE'S NOTHING I CAN DO ABOUT IT."

What if you could do something but choose not to? You're convinced that anything you do or say would make things worse or that the price for any action you might take is too high. In that case, write on your card: "I CHOOSE TO DO NOTHING."

But aren't you right back where you started? Far from it. Deciding not to act is far different from failing to decide. Decision brings peace.

4) Worry feeding on inertia

Oh, for heaven's sake! When are you going to seal the driveway? Make an appointment on the prayer card. Write down a rain date, too.

Now go to sleep.

5) Worry thriving on evasion

This is the toughest. It's so huge! Yet, you can't really know the full consequences of your decision either way.

Think of the major decisions you've made in your life. Did you have all the facts? Could you foresee exactly where your decision would lead you?

Ellen, Jeremiah and I learned as much as we could about Ellen's new job with the Madison Diocese, about local schools and parishes, about Wisconsin winters and what we could do to survive them. We knew what we were leaving, and we thought we knew how we'd feel about leaving it.

But I could never have foreseen all the consequences of a move from northern California to Wisconsin, a move from primary breadwinner to temporarily unemployed, a move from living an easy day's drive from family to being more than 2,000 miles away—the wrenching pain and regret, the challenge and growth, the joy and the strong sense that we had put ourselves exactly where God wanted us.

Isn't that the case with any major life decision?

Seen in this light, you really can't make a "wrong" decision. Whatever you choose, when you sincerely ask for God's guidance, you will grow in faith and love. You will experience triumph and failure, sorrow and joy. You will more fully know God's abiding love and grace.

So, *now* what are you worried about?

<*>

Five kinds of worry—and what to do about them

1. Worry thriving on ignorance: get the information you need

2. Worry lurking in the future: prepare as well as you can

3. Worry festering in the past: make amends if needed, then let go

4. Worry feeding on inertia: get into action

5. Worry thriving on evasion: ask for God's guidance, then decide

<*>

"Have no anxiety at all, but in everything, by prayer and petition, with thanksgiving, make your requests known to God. Then the peace of God that surpasses all understanding will guard your hearts and minds in Christ Jesus" (Phil 4:6–7).

---

10 How Are We to Pray?

If you're a parent, God has blessed you richly by letting you participate in creation. You experience the deepest joy and the sharpest pain life has to offer. You give your child your love, your time, your heart. You protect and teach that child, constantly preparing for the day when your precious offspring will go out into the world to make a life separate from you, outside your protection.

Your child may push you away, resent your corrections, protest your decisions, ignore your advice. This is as it must be. The child must struggle to be independent from the parent just as the chick must struggle to break through the eggshell. Often, the difficult child becomes the confident adult.

What if, after all your loving and caring and struggling, your man child or woman child never writes, never visits, phones only to ask for help or money or to blame you for anything that goes wrong? How would you feel? What would you say to such a child? Would you ever stop loving him or her?

Aren't we sometimes like that ungrateful child?

God has given us life and everything we need to live that life abundantly. Each day we awaken to his new creation and the endless possibilities of life in the Spirit. God is present for us in every living thing we encounter during that day.

Do we greet the gift of each new day with gratitude? Or do we only "phone home" when we want something or have a complaint or want to blame God for the rotten mess we feel our lives to be?

Are you still praying to Santa God?

As children, we may pray to Santa God, who "knows when we've been bad or good" and dispenses punishments and rewards as our conduct merits. But what if Santa God doesn't deliver? What if we say our prayers and mind our parents and follow all the rules, and Santa God doesn't bring the new bicycle or the baby brother or the passing grade on the math test? What does Santa God do when players on both teams pray for victory? Does the better prayer win?

Most of us stop praying to Santa God about the time we abandon Santa Claus. Some go on praying in the same old way but don't really expect an answer. Sadly, some stop praying at all.

Jesus taught us a new way to pray, first by telling us what not to do:

"In praying, do not babble like the pagans, who think that they will be heard because of their many words. Do not be like them. Your Father knows what you need before you ask him" (Mt 6:7–8).

Jesus taught us a new way to pray.

———— ‹•› ————

Then why pray at all? The answer is contained in the words of the prayer Jesus gave us:

Our Father in heaven,
hallowed be your name,
your kingdom come,
your will be done,
on earth as in heaven.
Give us today our daily bread;
and forgive us our debts,
as we forgive our debtors;
and do not subject us to the final test,
but deliver us from the evil one (Mt 6:9–13).

We pay homage to God (while calling him "Abba," or "Daddy"). We pray for sustenance, forgiveness, deliverance. We pray that God's will, not our own, be done. How many times have you said these words? Do you really mean them? How are you to know God's will for you?

Keith James, a deeply spiritual man living in Scottsdale Tasmania, Australia, shared with me the "dynamics of prayer for solving problems" attributed to Shoghi Effendi. I found that I had much to learn from this process, and I share it with you now as an aid to understanding God's will in your life.

1) We are to pray and meditate on the problem and then "remain in the silence of contemplation" for a few minutes.

I'd always been the pray-and-run type. I told God what I wanted. I thanked him for my blessings. (Well, on a good day, I thanked him.) Then I got on with my life. I've been teaching myself to wait, to listen, to let silence and quiet fill me. This isn't easy. Consciousness (what some people call "monkey mind") wants to fill the emptiness with word noise. When I can catch the monkey, I gently dismiss it and invite the silence back in.

"The Spirit too comes to the aid of our weakness; for we do not know how to pray as we ought, but the Spirit itself intercedes with inexpressible groanings" (Rom 8:26).

If the answer is to come for me that day, it comes quietly, in a soul stirring, perhaps with a voice that sounds very much like my own.

2) Don't judge the answer you receive. If the decision seems truly to have come in response to your prayer, hold to it. Determine that you will carry out your decision. This is not wish, not longing. It is specific future action. "When determination is born, immediately take the next step."

3) Have faith and confidence that "the power will flow through you, the right way will appear, the door will open, the right thought, the right message, the right principle, or the right book will be given you."

"Fear is useless," Jesus told the father of the little girl thought to be dead. "What is needed is trust" (cf. Mk 5:36).

4) As you rise from prayer, act as if your prayer has been answered. Be open to God's power and trust that he will act through you. If no words come, linger silently in God's presence, trusting that God knows your heart better than you know yourself.

My friend Jean Browman says she has a favorite prayer for the hard times:

"Thank you, Lord, for the opportunity. I sure hope you know what you're doing." I've modified it for my own use: "Thank you, Lord, for the opportunity. I sure hope you know what we're doing."

We need the Lord's Prayer, silence, and just two more words: "Thank you."

Thank you for life. Thank you for love. Thank you for healing.

Thank you in the dawn. Thank you in daylight. Thank you in darkness. Thank you in good times and bad, joy and sorrow.

Just this and nothing more: thank you.

"Do you not know that your body is a temple of the holy Spirit within you, whom you have from God, and that you are not your own?" (1 Cor 6:19).

---

11 Maintaining the Temple of the Spirit

If we want to come closer to God and gain the rich blessing of spiritual peace, we mustn't ignore the proper care and feeding of the body, the temple of the soul.

When your body cries out for rest, do you give it a donut and coffee instead? When you're anxious or frightened, do you "self-medicate" with nicotine or alcohol?

Eating right and getting enough exercise aren't punishments for disobedience. They are the path of physical well-being—just as God's commandments are the path of spiritual well-being.

God's commandments never change, but expert advice on diet and exercise keeps shifting on us. What we know for sure this week may be refuted by some new study next week.

A generation ago, nutritionists told us to eat slabs of beef and drink whole milk, "nature's most perfect food," by the quart. Now they tell us that such fare will clog our hearts.

Exercise gurus preached the doctrine "no pain/no gain." Then the pendulum swung the other way, and we were assured that "any exercise is better than no exercise." Now we seem to be back to a middle ground, with experts recommending thirty minutes of moderate exercise (anything from jogging to brisk housework) five days a week.

So what *should* we do?

The great baseball player Satchel Paige gave us these guidelines for healthy living:

"Avoid fried food which angry up the blood. If your stomach disputes you, lie down and pacify it with cooling thoughts. Keep the juice flowing by jangling around gently as you move. Go lightly on vices such as carrying on in society—the social ramble ain't restful" (Satchel Paige's *Rules for Right Living*).

Old Satch just might have been the greatest pitcher who ever lived. We'll never know for sure, since the barrier erected by racial prejudice kept Paige from pitching in the major leagues until he was well past what must have been an incredible prime. But his performance in the professional Negro Leagues and in exhibitions against the top white professionals indicate that he was unequaled in his—and perhaps any—day.

Paige kept pitching, day after day, year after year, without any of the benefits of modern sports medicine. He knew how to listen to his body and to give it what it needed.

Here's a quick rundown of what science has added to Paige's intuitions—ten moderate, common sense guidelines on diet and exercise:

1) Eat a diet rich in fresh fruits, veggies and whole grains.

2) Cut down on fat and sugar.

You can eat well on what my wife Ellen calls "the tree bark and prune diet." Dr. Art Ulene proved as much on a segment of *The Today Show.* He presented two seemingly identical sets of meals, one made with conventional ingredients, the other with low-or no-fat substitutes. The first set of meals contained 2,300 calories (not a bad total for a reasonably active adult), but fifty-five percent of those calories were derived from fat. By using the substitutes, Dr. Ulene cut the calories to 1,200. More significantly, only seven percent of those calories came from fat.

Hey—with that kind of cushion, I can still hit Jamie's Bakery for one of their incredible peanut butter chocolate chip cookies.

3) Eliminate nicotine, and cut down on or eliminate caffeine and alcohol. These are powerful, addictive drugs. They are also socially acceptable (nicotine less and less), so we tend to underestimate the effects they have on us.

4) Eat small portions several times a day rather than one or two large meals. "Grazing" is better for digestion and helps the body absorb and use nutrients.

5) Have your biggest meal when you get up and taper off until bedtime. Many do it backward, with little or no breakfast and a big dinner.

6) Don't eat anything substantial within two hours of bedtime. Digestion is an extremely active process and can disrupt sleep.

7) Find moderate forms of exercise that tone rather than tear down.

8) Exercise regularly, at least five days a week if possible. A little every day is much better than nothing all week and a lot on Saturday. By making exercise a habit, you'll eliminate the "should I or shouldn't I?" debate. (It's *so* easy to find reasons not to exercise.)

Build your endurance gradually. Find something that gets your body moving for a lifetime. Find activities you enjoy. Walking the mall with a friend "counts" as exercise, even if you have a great time. Vary your activities so you won't get too bored and so different muscle groups get a chance to work.

9) Exercise at about the same time every day.

You'll establish a healthy pattern, and after a few weeks, your energy will show up right when you need it.

10) Don't exercise within two hours of bedtime.

Exercise elevates your heart rate and metabolism. That's great for conditioning and weight maintenance but not so good for trying to fall asleep.

But aren't we already eating better and exercising more these days?

Apparently not. We just *read* healthier.

It's hard to pick up a magazine or "lifestyle" section of the newspaper without running into a feature on proper diet. But "ten ways to use tofu on your Thanksgiving table" will be surrounded by ads for all the tasty, fatty stuff and recipes for how to make them even tastier—and fattier. As a society, we keep getting fatter, and our percentage of body fat keeps going up.

As with diet, likewise with exercise. We talk a good workout, while Jane Fonda and Richard Simmons get our exercise for us.

Be gentle and patient with yourself.
But keep working at it.

———<◆>———

"Watch and pray that you may not undergo the test. The spirit is willing, but the flesh is weak" (Mt 26:41).

It's hard to break habits, especially when they get tangled up with emotional needs—as diet and exercise often do. It's hard to find time to add something new to a life already overfilled, especially when that something promises to be painful or difficult or both. Be gentle and patient with yourself. But keep working at it.

Read all you can; listen to the "experts"; keep up with the latest theories.

Listen to your own body and bring your questions and doubts to God in prayer.

<♦>

Ten guidelines for healthy living

1. Eat a diet rich in fresh fruits, veggies and whole grains.

2. Cut down on fat and sugar.

3. Eliminate nicotine, and go easy on caffeine and alcohol.

4. Eat small portions several times a day rather than one or two large meals.

5. Have your biggest meal when you get up and taper off until bedtime.

6. Don't eat anything substantial within two hours of bedtime.

7. Find moderate forms of exercise that tone rather than tear down.

8. Exercise regularly.

9. Exercise at about the same time every day.

10. Don't exercise within two hours of bedtime.

<♦>

"When they take you before...rulers and authorities, do not worry about how or what your defense will be or about what you are to say. For the holy Spirit will teach you at that moment what you should say" (Lk 12:11–12).

12 Five Ways to Get Worry to Work for You

Imagine that tomorrow you must give a speech to several hundred strangers. Does the prospect make your palms sweat and your throat dry up? You're not alone. Opinion polls reveal that Americans fear public speaking more than anything else—illness, poverty and even death.

Let's use America's Number One Fear to illustrate five more important principles for getting worry to work for you.

1) Let work replace worry.

Overpreparation can displace much of your anxiety. Research your speech thoroughly; write it out carefully, and practice delivering it to a sympathetic friend, your dog or cat, or even the bathroom mirror. Practice over breakfast, on the way to work, and between appointments. When the speech is as good as you can possibly make it, practice it twice more.

2) Visualize.

As the time of the speech approaches, this exciting movie may start playing in the theater of your mind:

"Speaker makes idiot of self / audience riots in protest." If so, book a new movie: "Speaker has rapt audience hanging on every word." Picture yourself giving your speech perfectly. See your audience listening intently.

3) Get out of the way.

Not all of you is afraid, just the ego part, which worries about what others think of you. Gently tell your frightened ego, "This isn't about you." Concentrate on what you want to say. Think about what the listeners need and want. What will they get for spending their time listening to you? How will your speech make their lives better?

When your ego cries for attention, gently tell it again, "This isn't about you." If you think about your audience and not about yourself, you'll turn worry into constructive energy.

4) Let God guide you.

Every time I'm privileged to give a talk, lead a workshop, or read the Word at Mass, I recite the end of Psalm 19:

"Let the words of my mouth meet with your favor; keep the thoughts of my heart before you, Lord, my rock and my redeemer" (Ps 19:15).

I got in the habit after learning that one of my heroes, sportscaster Red Barber, used this simple prayer before going on the air. It has never let me down.

5) Imagine a sympathetic audience.

Do you go to Mass hoping for a rotten sermon? Of course not. You want the priest to succeed; you want to be informed and enriched. Most of the folks in your audience feel the same way. They're pulling for you. They may bring a "show me" attitude, but they'll give you the benefit of the doubt, or they wouldn't have shown up in the first place.

Assume you're talking to people who want to hear what you have to say. Be gentle with yourself.

You can choose not to worry. If you do, you can reclaim your life, releasing energy and joy you didn't know you had. You know this. You've prepared, visualized and prayed. Still, when the moment comes to step behind the podium and begin speaking, you find yourself shaking, with head spinning and stomach churning. You're ready to abandon hope.

Don't. We all get anxious at such moments. Stop worrying about worrying. Gently lead yourself back into the presence of God.

"I sought the Lord, who answered me, delivered me from all my fears" (Ps 34:5).

If your mind insists on showing disaster films of failure, patiently change the tape and cue up the new success feature.

Your ego is like a frightened child, alone and bewildered by shimmering shadows and strange noises. Embrace that poor child, as you would your own frightened son or daughter. Tell your child, "Don't be afraid. I'll take care of you." Then listen for your loving Father, telling you the same thing.

<◆>

If you're worried about speaking to others:

1. Let work replace worry.

2. Visualize.

3. Get out of the way.

4. Let God guide you.

5. Imagine a sympathetic audience.

<◆>

"If I speak in human and angelic tongues but do not have love, I am a resounding gong or a clashing cymbal" (1 Cor 13:1).

---

13   On the Next Oprah...Me!
—A Chance to Practice What I Preach

"Hi. My name is Angie, and I'm calling for the Oprah Show."

My bluff had been called.

I teach workshops on publishing. When we talk about ways for authors to help promote their books—including participation on talk shows—I often joke that, "Oprah hasn't called me yet."

Now Oprah was calling, or not Oprah exactly, but Angie, one of a cadre of bright young producers who put the nationally syndicated *Oprah Winfrey Show* together each day.

"We're doing a program on 'how to avoid losing your cool,'" Angie told me, "and we want you to be one of the guests. It's next Tuesday."

"Yes. I'd be available next Tuesday," said a voice sounding something like mine, only a lot higher and squeakier.

All this came about because of a book I wrote called *Slow Down—And Get More Done*, techniques for handling stress. I turned the book into a workshop. I got interviewed by telephone for radio call-in shows all over the United States and

Canada. I went on a network television affiliate in Madison
and on cable TV with Sylvia in Sheboygan. So I'd done a lot
of talking on the subject, and the thought of microphones
and even camera lenses didn't scare me too much.

But Oprah!

Actually, I didn't have much time to be nervous. Angie
and her cohorts left nothing to chance, calling several times
a day to go over my segment of the show.

The anxiety didn't really hit me until I was on the Inter-
state, Chicago bound, and it occurred to me that Oprah's
audience was probably considerably bigger than the one for
Sylvia in Sheboygan. I started breathing deeply to calm
myself and almost hyperventilated.

"Thank you for this opportunity, Lord," I prayed. "I
hope you know what we're doing."

The anxiety passed. It always does. But every time the
word "Oprah" floated through my consciousness, my stomach took a rude tumble.

As I drove into nightfall and the suburbs of Chicago, I
couldn't remember any of the points I'd prepared to make.
What if I went blank while on camera?

God had given me a wonderful opportunity to practice
all I've been preaching about conquering anxiety.

I checked in at my hotel, had my dinner, took a walk.
Then I took out one of my oversized yellow notecards and a
magic marker and boiled my thoughts down to four or five
key reminder words. I studied the list, covered it, recited the
words, then checked myself against it. I rehearsed various
phrasings, but I didn't try to memorize specific language. I
visualized myself, smiling and confident, trading quips with
Oprah on camera while the audience laughed and applauded. Then I prayed that God would cleanse my spirit,
guide my steps, and give me the words I needed.

I managed to fall asleep but woke up well before dawn.

The lights of Chicago shone brightly ou
studied my card. I tried to get back i
dressed, and went for my morning jog. .
Michigan Avenue, I tried to rehearse my ɪ
found that I couldn't remember the key wc
Now I was certain I was going to draw a bl____ ...amera.
A limo picked me up and took me from the hotel to the
studios of Harpo Productions for makeup and briefings in
the "green room." While I waited for my segment of the
show, I chatted with the makeup man. I could hear the
audience applaud and laugh just down the hall. I watched
the monitor, fascinated by the notion that the show I was
watching—along with millions of other people—was actually happening only a few feet away.

The strange and wonderful thing that happened to me
on the Oprah Show then began.

I watched some of the world's self-professed most impa-
tient people talking about how they cut in line at movies and
ran red lights. I listened intently, becoming absorbed. I
became especially concerned for a woman named Marlene,
who described how she had once nearly injured one of her
children when she pulled away from the curb before the kid
had gotten all the way into the car. The audience roared, as
if she'd told a great joke. Marlene laughed with them, but I
thought she looked uneasy and unhappy underneath the
forced smile.

As I thought about Marlene, I stopped thinking about me.

A producer came for me. I grabbed my yellow card as
she led me into the center ring of a little circus, with the
audience in bleachers all around. Oprah herself stood across
the center ring, microphone in hand, waiting for her cue.

Things began to move fast. My heart pounded, but I was
hardly aware of my body. I said a final silent prayer as Oprah
introduced me. She called me "a recovering speedaholic."

wasn't nervous any more. In fact, I felt unusually calm. remembered all the points I had planned to make—and decided not to make them. Instead, I turned to face Marlene, smiled and began to talk. I don't remember exactly what I said, but it was something like: "We're always in such a hurry to get to the next place. But life isn't really about getting to the next place. Life is right here, right now."

We went into a commercial. I wondered if all those producers would attack me for not sticking to the plan. I glanced at Oprah. She nodded and seemed to mouth the words "Good job."

"She might toss it back to you for some final tips," one of the producers whispered to me just before the end of the final commercial break.

I looked up at one of the teleprompters over the cameras and watched the lettering spell out: "MARSHALL ARE THERE ANY FINAL TIPS FOR US?" As I finished reading, I heard Oprah saying, "Marshall, are there any final tips for us?"

I gave my tip about taking several "mini vacations" every day. Folks applauded. The lights over the cameras went out. Another producer led me back to the green room. I hadn't had a fifteen full minutes of fame, but I'd had plenty.

Marlene came up to me as I gathered my coat and my genuine "Oprah Show" coffee mug.

"Are you really a recovering speedaholic?" she asked, looking at me intently.

"Something like that," I said.

She nodded, smiled. "Then maybe there's hope for me," she said.

She wasn't playing to the audience, now. Something I'd said had helped.

My appearance on Oprah wasn't about me. It was about Marlene—and anybody else God had given me to talk with that day.

"But to you who hear I say, love your enemies, do good to those who hate you" (Lk 6:27).

---

14 Don't Get Mad. Don't Get Even. Get Peace.

While hanging in agony on the cross, Jesus asked his Father to forgive those who had crucified him. If that had been the end of this incredible story—if Christ had never risen from the dead, never appeared to the apostles, never sent the Spirit to sustain us until he comes again—we would remember and revere him anyway, for that final astounding act of forgiveness.

He tells us to forgive just as he did. He gave us the parable of the foolish servant, who refuses to forgive his debtors but expects forgiveness from his master, and he told us to ask the Father to forgive our sins "as we forgive those who sin against us."

How many times are we to forgive? Seven? Jesus said not seven, not even seventy times seven. That was his way of saying always, every time.

Imagine what the world would be like if everyone truly lived by this precept. The divorce rate would plunge. Violent crime would subside. Peace and harmony would reign. The lion would truly lie down with the lamb.

We'll probably never suffer the way Christ and the martyrs suffered, with public humiliation and painful death. But the next time you sit down to relax at the end of a long, hard day, the phone may ring. If it does, you'll rush to pick it up, only to be told that you may have already won a fabulous recreational flotation device and need send only three easy monthly payments of $24.95 to claim your free prize. You'll feel annoyed.

Next time you go out to eat, your waiter may indeed keep you waiting, may get your order mixed up with somebody else's, and may even insist that you really *did* order what he brought you. You might feel too annoyed to enjoy your meal.

If you take in a movie after dinner, the person behind you may give away the plot. You can keep quiet and have your movie ruined or speak up and have your movie ruined. Either way, you'll feel angry.

On your way back to your car after the movie, someone may pull up, open the car door, and empty a full ashtray onto the ground. You'll be outraged.

Finally, as you drive home, your evening ruined, someone may cut you off in traffic, causing you to brake so hard your neck aches for a week.

These are minor annoyances, to be sure, especially compared to death on the cross, but enough to keep us in a state of anxiety and anger—if we let them.

Forgive? Sure. But first you have to *teach that idiot a lesson*, right? Besides, that lousy, inattentive, uncaring driver is simply the last straw, one too many aggravations. So you honk your horn, yell and shake your fist. And you feel better, right?

Wrong.

You simply become somebody else's idiot. The other driver, who is probably just as good a driver as you are, is now ready to yell at the next person who gets in *his* way.

Or maybe the other driver doesn't even notice your tirade. It only affects you—and the effect on you isn't good. Rather than releasing your anger, your tantrum feeds on itself. You get more angry, more tense, more anxious. Once again, God's instruction is for our own good. Forgive, and *you* will be healed, by the very process of forgiving.

But you didn't just want to teach a lesson. You wanted to punish the evildoer for his sin! That isn't your job. It's God's.

"Do not look for revenge...for it is written, 'Vengeance is mine, I will repay, says the Lord'" (Rom 12:19).

Forgive, and you will be healed,
by the very process of forgiving.

————◂◆▸————

Is forgiveness really possible for mere mortals like us, in the heat of the daily battle? Isn't all that yelling and gesturing and horn honking a natural reaction, like sneezing or coughing or laughing? For years I assumed that anger is a force of nature, a "natural" reaction, and that stifling such natural reactions is unhealthy.

With prayer and practice, I'm coming to realize that the adrenaline rush is natural, but I can choose what to do with that rush. I can cut off the anger, take a breath, pray, remind myself that Christ is present in the other as surely as he is in me. On a good day, I can laugh at myself and my anger. On a *really* good day, I can thank God that the momentary lapse didn't cause an accident, and I can even smile, say "God bless you" and mean it.

When I do, I can feel my body and my mind calm down. The more I do it, the more "natural" this sort of reaction becomes and the faster the adrenaline surge subsides.

I don't succeed every time, of course. When I'm tired and in a hurry (they always go together, don't they?), I slide back into old anger. But I succeed more than I fail, and if I can do it, so can you.

Some of my students are a lot better at this sort of radical forgiveness than I am. At one workshop recently, when we discussed the parking-lot-as-ashtray vexation, a woman offered a wonderful solution that hadn't even occurred to me.

She told us she had started carrying a hand broom, a dustpan, and a paper bag in the car. When she came on the carnage of cigarette butts, she simply got out her kit and cleaned up the mess.

Not fair, you say? She didn't make the mess, so why should she have to clean it up? She didn't *have* to clean it up. She volunteered. She got rid of the offensive filth, and she felt good about herself, all for a few seconds' of sweeping.

One time, as she bent to her task, she heard someone walk up behind her.

"Sorry," a deep voice said. "I wasn't thinking. Let me."

A man took the broom and pan and cleaned up after himself. Then they both went away feeling good. That sounds a lot better than fuming about the mess and leaving it to discourage and anger others.

We are called to *love*, not just tolerate

Jesus asks for more than civility, more than tolerance. He asks us to *love* our enemies, to "do good to those who hate you." Listen to the rest:

"Bless those who curse you, pray for those who mistreat you. To the person who strikes you on one cheek, offer the other one as well, and from the person who takes your cloak, do not withhold even your tunic. Give to everyone who asks of you, and from the one who takes what is yours do not demand it back" (Lk 6:28–30).

I grew up believing that a real man never backs down. I've had a hard time reconciling John Wayne with Jesus Christ. But in the end, there's just no escaping "Do to others as you would have them do to you" (Lk 6:31), or "Bless those who persecute [you], bless and do not curse them.... Do not repay anyone evil for evil; be concerned for what is noble in the sight of all. If possible, on your part, live at peace with all. Beloved, do not look for revenge.... Do not be conquered by evil but conquer evil with good" (Rom 12:14–21).

It's not enough to refrain from punching our brother or sister in the nose. We must *love* them. Listen to these words from 1 John 2:10–11:

"Whoever loves his brother remains in the light, and there is nothing in him to cause a fall. Whoever hates his brother is in darkness; he walks in darkness and does not know where he is going because the darkness has blinded his eyes."

Again in 1 John 3:14–15: "Whoever does not love remains in death. Everyone who hates his brother is a murderer, and you know that no murderer has eternal life remaining in him."

We may not *feel* like loving a person whom we believe has offended us. That's all right. We need time to work through the emotions, especially for hurts that run deep. Forgiveness doesn't mean denying our feelings or allowing ourselves to become passive victims. Forgiveness may even require that we approach the "offender" to confront the situation. In doing this, we are to act out of Christian love, not a desire for revenge.

This is the higher way, the Jesus way, the way of peace and light.

"We know that all things work for good for those who love God, who are called according to his purpose" (Rom 8:28).

---

15 Seeking Mercy Instead of Justice

If we lived blameless lives, we wouldn't have any regrets. "Justice will bring about peace; right will produce calm and security" (Is 32:17).

But as Paul reminds us, "all have sinned" (Rom 3:23). We must leave our gifts at the altar and be reconciled with those we've hurt (cf. Mt 5:24). We must open ourselves to God's amazing love, learn our lessons, and let it go.

What about the bad things others have done to us? We are to forgive—with our actions and in our hearts—for our own good, so that we may leave the bitterness behind and walk in God's light.

We must open ourselves to God's amazing love.

———<◆>———

But what if you can't find anybody to blame—yourself or anybody else—for the sorrow in your life? What if you're mad at God? How are you to reconcile God's love for you with the pain he seems to be inflicting on you?

Much has been written to explain why bad things happen to good people (namely *us*, right?). Philosophy and history as well as religion have tried to explain, if not justify, the existence of such evil in the world.

There can be no good without evil, some say. How would you know pleasure if you didn't experience pain, or know joy without sorrow? Perhaps only suffering can enable us to understand the sufferings of others and to react with empathy and compassion. True enough, but scant comfort when you're living in the pain.

Many years ago, my wife was told she had colon cancer and must undergo surgery immediately. Ellen handled the news well, learning all she could and taking responsibility for her recovery. I held up all right—until they wheeled Ellen into the elevator to take her up to surgery. As the doors closed, my legs dissolved. I staggered and fell against the wall. Searing pain ripped my chest, and hot tears stung my eyes. Raw fear and grief tore through my faith.

Ellen came through the surgery beautifully (and has been cancer-free since, thank God). She faced her convalescence with courage, more concerned for me than for herself.

When she got well enough to get out of bed, I walked with her down the corridor onto the next ward, which happened to be the maternity ward. As we looked through the window at the babies in their bassinets, I began to weep. Ellen tried to console me (the one there to cheer *her* up, right?) as sorrow and rage overwhelmed me.

It was so unfair! Ellen is a caring, loving Christian. More than anything in life, she wanted another child after the birth of our son, Jeremiah. Others got the children, and she got cancer.

Our suffering ultimately deepened our faith and strengthened the bond that unites us. I hope it made us more caring, empathetic Christians. But at the time it just hurt—hurt so much, I wasn't sure I'd be able to bear it.

Ellen had to fight the notion that she must have done something awful to have deserved to get cancer. Over and over, I told her that she wasn't to blame. Besides, I reasoned, what kind of God would give cancer to her—or anybody else—as a punishment? But if God didn't give her cancer, had he simply washed his celestial hands of such matters and left Ellen to suffer from an unlucky toss of the genetic dice? How are we to understand such suffering and reconcile it with a loving God of justice and compassion?

Is it fair that Ellen got cancer? No! My soul rages against the notion that she "deserved" her disease. But is it fair that she recovered while cancer killed our friend Denise, leaving a grieving husband and two small children? No. That's not fair either.

Is it fair that I was born in a country blessed with freedom and abundant natural resources, that I have a loving wife and son, live in a warm house, have plenty of food and even the luxury of satisfying work to do? Did I somehow deserve to be born into my life instead of a life spent fighting disease and starvation day after hopeless day?

I don't remember passing a qualifying test. Do you?

Maybe we're asking the wrong question, making the wrong demand on God. Perhaps it isn't justice we should seek, but rather, mercy.

Job dares to question the fairness of a God who would rain down disaster on his good and faithful servant. Job's sense of justice is outraged! The wicked, not the righteous, should get the boils and plagues.

When at last he is allowed to confront God with his complaint, God answers his question with a bigger question.

"Where were you when I laid the foundation of the earth?...
Tell me, if you have understanding" (Jb 38:4).

> Have you ever in your lifetime commanded the morning
> and shown the dawn its place
> For taking hold of the ends of the earth,
> till the wicked are shaken from its surface?...
> Have you entered into the sources of the sea,
> or walked about in the depths of the abyss?
> Have the gates of death been shown to you,
> or have you seen the gates of darkness?
> (Jb 38:12–13, 16–17).

Well, *have* you?

God's ways are not our ways. We cannot understand his plan for the universe. Like Job, we can see only a tiny part of creation. We are stuck in space and time, trapped in frail bodies, limited in our ability to perceive and process experience. God is timeless and infinite. God sees what we cannot—that our time on earth is but a brief portion of our spirit journey.

Life doesn't make sense; it isn't fair. It isn't fair in the bad times, when we question God's wisdom and justice. And *it is no more fair in the good times*, when God's special favor seems to be poured out on us.

We need to pray for God's guidance and open our souls to the Spirit to sustain us *in all times*. We need to do our best to live by God's precepts. We need to ask God to give us a keen awareness of our sins, so we may turn away from them and allow God to bring us closer to perfection. When we do this, God will deliver us from our anxieties, even in the midst of the raging storm.

"Can any of you by worrying add a single moment to your life-span?" (Mt 6:27).

16 Accepting the Inevitable

Worry can hurt you. It can strip you of your defenses against disease, rob you of rest, steal your serenity, your peace, your joy.

But God doesn't want us to worry. He has told us so.

"The Lord will guard you from all evil, will always guard your life.

The Lord will guard your coming and going both now and forever" (Ps 121:7–8).

God doesn't want us to worry.

————◆————

You've probably heard the serenity prayer. Perhaps you incorporate it into your daily prayer. Let's take another look at it now:

God grant me the serenity
To accept the things I cannot change,
The courage to change the things I can,
And the wisdom to know the difference.

Learning what is and what isn't within our control is the first step. Then we must learn to accept those things we can't control.

I learned a lot about acceptance from an old Schnauzer named Hilda. After Dad died, Mom "adopted" Hilda from the local hairdresser, and they looked after each other as best they could.

When Mom moved from California to Madison to be near my wife and me, she of course brought Hilda with her. (I say "of course" because that's just the way my family is. When we make a commitment to an animal, it's until death—ours or the animal's—do us part.)

I remember grabbing the pet carrier as it thudded onto the luggage carousel at the Madison airport and lugging Hilda outside for her first sniff of Wisconsin air. When I opened the cage door, I encountered the most woeful-looking critter I've ever seen. Poor old Hilda had fouled herself, and she was shaking with fear. Her legs wobbled so much that she could barely support herself as she stumbled out and took her first tentative steps into her new life.

I reached out a hand to her. She looked at me through watery eyes, decided I was a friend, and licked my fingers. Then she looked around and heaved a sigh, as if to say, "Okay. This is home now. What's next?"

She lived out that simple philosophy every day, even as advancing age left her increasingly unsteady on her feet and unsure of her bearings. She simply did her best with what remained to her, enjoying her food, keeping us good company, and rolling around in the sunshine on a patch of dirt in her yard.

It seems to be in the dog's nature to accept life as it comes. Here's how the writer Ambrose Bierce defined the dog: "He toils not, neither does he spin, yet Solomon in all his glory never lay upon a door mat all day long, sun-soaked and fly-fed and fat, while his master worked for the means wherewith to purchase an idle wag of the Solomonic tail, seasoned with a look of tolerant recognition."

I've met many people who embodied courage and acceptance, too, prime among them a remarkable woman named Olga. Advancing age, blindness and the ravages of disease and many operations could not conquer her indomitable spirit and genuine joy in living. The last time Olga went to the hospital, the doctor warned her she might not survive the surgery.

"Well, don't be so sad about it," Olga assured him. "Either I'll survive and have more life, which is wonderful, or I'll die and meet Jesus face to face, which is even more wonderful."

Olga would win either way.

I met another example of indomitable spirit the first time I saw Chuck Wheeler. He was lying on his back, preparing to bench press an enormous amount of weight. He had the thick muscles and sharp definition of a dedicated body builder. He wore glasses with dark lenses, even inside the gym, and his T-shirt carried the inscription, "Here comes Old Deadeye." He propped up his white cane against the Universal machine.

Chuck appeared at my office a few weeks later. He had a story to tell, and he thought I might be able to help him write it.

A few years back, he had been in a boating accident. As he and his friends were returning to a pier one night, the skipper, who had been drinking, mistook a light from a house for the dock light. He gunned the engine and rammed the boat into the pier. Chuck's two friends died, and he was blinded. He endured a long, difficult convalescence, during which his wife divorced him. Excruciating headaches plagued him as he tried to adjust to a new world of darkness.

He nearly went insane with rage at the unfairness of what had happened to him.

As he told the story, simply and without a trace of self-pity, a student appeared in my office doorway, saw that I was busy, and started to leave.

"Come on in, Cindy," Chuck said before I could acknowledge her presence. "We're about done."

Chuck left some of his work for me to read, flashed a killer smile at Cindy, and left. Cindy took his place in the chair across the desk from me.

"How did he know it was you?" I blurted out.

"Oh, he does that all the time," she said. "I thought it was my perfume, but he says he can recognize my footstep."

Chuck and I met often to discuss his writing. Actually, the biggest problem he was having involved knowing when he had reached the bottom of a page. We solved this with a simple attachment for the typewriter.

As we chatted, I learned that he had custody of a nine-year-old son, and together they were building an addition onto his house!

Chuck moved to Oregon and I to Wisconsin, but I remembered him over the years. I was delighted when I read a review in the *New York Times Book Review* of a first novel titled *Snakewalk*. Chuck had written his book! I ran out to get a copy and renewed my acquaintance with a courageous man who had accepted his circumstances and focused, not on what had been taken from him, but on what remained.

Not what I want, Father....

Remember Shadrach, Meshach, and Abednego, as they faced King Nebuchadnezzar's fiery furnace? (as described in Daniel 3:19–29). They refused to worship the king's golden idol, pledging to follow their God *even if he didn't save them from death.* They didn't bargain with God. ("We'll believe in you if you save us.") Their faith didn't depend on circumstances. They were ready to accept either outcome—painful death or miraculous redemption—with equal faith.

Mary, the mother of our Savior, didn't bargain with God either. In the first chapter of Luke's Gospel we read that she was "much perplexed" by the appearance of an angel, who told her that she would conceive and bear a son who would reign over the house of Jacob forever.

Mary didn't argue. She didn't bargain. She didn't ask for guarantees. She simply said, "I am the handmaid of the Lord. May it be done to me according to your word" (Lk 1:38).

When Jesus prayed in the Garden of Gethsemane the night the soldiers came for him, he felt "sorrow and distress" (cf. Mt 26:36). He asked his Father, "if it is possible, let this cup pass from me." But Jesus said with his next breath, "yet, not as I will, but as you will."

He had to endure the additional sorrow of finding his friends asleep, unable to support him with their presence as his trial on the cross drew near. Yet twice more he prayed, "My Father, if this cannot pass unless I drink it, your will be done." Jesus accepted his Father's will for him, however terrifying the consequences.

Through experience, prayer and Scripture study, we learn to discern what we can change and what we cannot. In God we find the courage to confront the things we can change and to accept the things we cannot change. With this acceptance comes inner peace.

"Do not worry about tomorrow; tomorrow will take care of itself. Sufficient for a day is its own evil" (Mt 6:34).

*"Come to me, all you who labor and are burdened, and I will
give you rest. Take my yoke upon you and learn from me, for I
am meek and humble of heart; and you will find rest for
yourselves. For my yoke is easy, and my burden light"* (Mt
11:28–30).

---

17 Surrendering to Faith/Fear

Pauline was struggling with her faith. She sought the
help of a spiritual advisor but found herself fighting his
advice.

"As I sat in front of him, arrogantly telling him once
again that everything he had to say was a crock, he responded, 'Your ego does not like letting go of the idea that
you are the center of the universe.'"

Pauline sat for months in the midst of her doubts, "feeling my faithlessness, taking it in silence, feeling it fully." She
calls it "a terrible and perhaps necessary journey," for "it
is only when life begins to emerge from the void that
one knows the fertility of that void. Faith and angst go
together."

"How could we go through something like that without
anxiety?" she concludes. "How can such endeavor be without
anxiety and pain? It hurts to let go of what we think we are."

This faith, she concluded, is "beyond description. It just is."

I have been overwhelmed by pain and uncertainty and
anguish. I'm sure you have, too. "I can't go on," the soul
wails. "I give up." But life doesn't let you give up.

Somehow in these painful moments of complete surrender, I've felt a peace I cannot understand. Nothing in my

circumstances has changed. The universe remains indifferent to my pain. But I feel God's presence in the midst of my fear. How can this be?

In such moments, I experience a kind of death and rebirth. The "I" who thinks he is at the center of creation and in charge of salvation dies in this moment. I sense the awakening of the Spirit within. Faith is reborn. This rebirth scares me because it opens me to new possibilities. If I surrender to this fear, I feel the exhilaration of walking with Christ.

Our culture encourages us to run away from such intense inner experience. This is a great mistake. Without this faith/fear, we'll never grow in the spirit. Faith/fear isn't the enemy. It's a sign that wonderful things are about to happen, are happening, within us.

Stand still. Let faith/fear wash through you.

I once stood in the carport of my brother's apartment in Phoenix and watched lightning fill the summer sky. I had never seen such energy. For me, the experience of letting faith/fear flood through me feels like having that desert storm inside of me. No wonder I spent so much of my life trying to evade it!

I no longer try to make the storm go away; it simply passes, leaving behind a calm much deeper than the time before the storm. I have faced the fear, surrendered to it. I have survived and am unharmed. Now what do I need to fear?

"Darkness is not dark for you, and night shines as the day. Darkness and light are but one" (Ps 139:12).

Now I can at last embrace the paradox of fear in faith. I can recognize my faith/fear, let go and trust God.

Nurture faith/fear by being mindful of God's presence in everyone and everything. Then you will know the truth of the central paradox of our faith:

"For whoever wishes to save his life will lose it, but whoever loses his life for my sake will find it" (Mt 16:25). Having let yourself be consumed by fear, you are reborn in faith/fear and can claim your truth in the Scriptures: "The Lord is with me; I am not afraid; what can mortals do against me?" (Ps 118:6).

You will have always the promise Jesus made to the disciples before he ascended into heaven: "Go, therefore, and make disciples of all nations, baptizing them in the name of the Father, and of the Son, and of the Holy Spirit, teaching them to observe all that I have commanded you. And behold, I am with you always, until the end of the age" (Mt 28:19–20).

"The beginning of wisdom is the fear of the Lord, and knowledge of the Holy One is understanding" (Prv 9:10).

18 Living Faith/Fear on a Cold Day in January

As I write these words, the latest political scandal is playing itself out in Washington. Meanwhile, brutal cold and snow have afflicted much of the Midwest, and unseasonal tornadoes have hit parts of the South, while California waits for that big earthquake that has been so long predicted. People are wondering if the new millennium will bring, if not the end of the world, at least a global computer crash.

We will never eliminate stress from our lives. Our struggle with fear and anxiety never ends. We must fight it every day, getting all the help we can.

When Jesus went into the desert to fast and pray, Satan tempted him three times. Each time, Jesus drove Satan away by citing Scripture. But that didn't end the struggle. Jesus faced many more tests, culminating in the agony in Gethsemane and the torture on the cross.

On this bitterly cold January day, I seek refuge in the Eucharistic Celebration at the campus Catholic Center near my office. The noontime regulars have shared a great deal with one another over the years. Through their petitions,

I've learned about many of the burdens they carry, the pain they bear, and the anxiety they cope with.

This day our pastor shocks us with a petition of his own, for the soul of one of our brothers. Richard Schoenherr has died in the night, two days short of his 61st birthday. We pray for Richard, for our sense of loss and the loss to the church and university communities. We pray, too, for ourselves and the tenuous nature of our lives on earth.

We share a somber Eucharist. I return to work saddened but strengthened. I open my e-mail to a message from Tim, a member of a sort of "cyber-congregation" of spiritual seekers.

"I am not the electric company," Tim has written, "just a light bulb." Intrigued, I read on.

"I had to abandon myself some time ago and bet my life on this Godthing," he went on. He said he found the journey "... more wonderful than I could have imagined. Terrifying at times but wonderful."

Yes, he felt terror. "The fear is always based in my forgetfulness or unbelief," he said.

I realize I've bet my life on the "Godthing," too. Even if you could somehow "prove" to me that Jesus never rose from the dead, that it was all just a pretty story, or a hoax perpetuated by zealous disciples, or a mighty myth, I'd still put my money on what Jesus taught and how he lived.

My big brother, Dale, has also posted a message. He is struggling to cope with a job that seems more and more capable of killing his spirit, as well as his body.

"I'm really having a tough time admitting that I am in over my head, over-committed," he writes. "Why do we have to get gut pains to wake up to the fact we should be asking for—nay, yelling for—help?"

He is moving slowly, painfully, toward making a difficult decision. Should he grind it out until the promised security of retirement, or quit the job—shedding the stress and re-claiming his life—but also abandoning financial security? The dilemma leads him into deep reflection.

"Shouldn't a human being, the creature with the most restless and searching mind, not be subject to change?" he challenges himself. "Why do we assume we are duty-bound to pick one career in life and follow it to its end?...

"I sometimes catch my little voice saying, 'this is the time allowed for a shower and it is a pleasant sensation; enjoy it instead of thinking about a million less pleasant things....'"

That little voice would lead him to quit the killer job. He got another job, with less stress and less money. (Why do the two always seem to run together in our society?) So far he's happy with his decision.

We don't get to the top of this mountain. We must rejoice in the climb and enjoy the view along the way.

————<♦>————

Is Dale through agonizing? Is Tim through being scared? Have I conquered my anxiety once and forever?

Nope, nope, and nope. Life isn't like that. We don't get to the top of this mountain. We must rejoice in the climb and enjoy the view along the way.

All of the pain and anxiety of this world will one day pass away, but God's love will endure forever.

As I walk home later that afternoon, I again receive the image of Jesus the Good Shepherd and, with it, this Scripture:

"Do not be afraid any longer, little flock, for your Father is pleased to give you the kingdom" (Lk 12:32).

I see my home at the end of the road. The light is on. Ellen is waiting for me.

auline
BOOKS & MEDIA

The Daughters of St. Paul operate book and media centers at the following addresses. Visit, call or write the one nearest you today, or find us on the World Wide Web, www.pauline.org

CALIFORNIA
3908 Sepulveda Blvd., Culver City, CA 90230; 310-397-8676
5945 Balboa Ave., San Diego, CA 92111; 619-565-9181
46 Geary Street, San Francisco, CA 94108; 415-781-5180

FLORIDA
145 S.W. 107th Ave., Miami, FL 33174; 305-559-6715

HAWAII
1143 Bishop Street, Honolulu, HI 96813; 808-521-2731
Neighbor Islands call: 800-259-8463

ILLINOIS
172 North Michigan Ave., Chicago, IL 60601; 312-346-4228

LOUISIANA
4403 Veterans Memorial Blvd., Metairie, LA 70006; 504-887-7631

MASSACHUSETTS
Rte. 1, 885 Providence Hwy., Dedham, MA 02026; 781-326-5385

MISSOURI
9804 Watson Rd., St. Louis, MO 63126; 314-965-3512

NEW JERSEY
561 U.S. Route 1, Wick Plaza, Edison, NJ 08817; 732-572-1200

NEW YORK
150 East 52nd Street, New York, NY 10022; 212-754-1110
78 Fort Place, Staten Island, NY 10301; 718-447-5071

OHIO
2105 Ontario Street, Cleveland, OH 44115; 216-621-9427

PENNSYLVANIA
9171-A Roosevelt Blvd., Philadelphia, PA 19114; 215-676-9494

SOUTH CAROLINA
243 King Street, Charleston, SC 29401; 843-577-0175

TENNESSEE
4811 Poplar Ave., Memphis, TN 38117; 901-761-2987

TEXAS
114 Main Plaza, San Antonio, TX 78205; 210-224-8101

VIRGINIA
1025 King Street, Alexandria, VA 22314; 703-549-3806

CANADA
3022 Dufferin Street, Toronto, Ontario, Canada M6B 3T5; 416-781-9131
1155 Yonge Street, Toronto, Ontario, Canada M4T 1W2; 416-934-3440

¡También somos su fuente para libros, videos y música en español!